D0262816

Nightmare On Green Street

MAY ALL YOUR MARS BARS
BE MERRY, BRIGHT & EDIBLE

B_ig MIKE
& LITTLE MIKE

Billy-Blagg
aka Peter Stone

Nightmare On Green Street

**Billy Blagg and Friends from
westhamonline.net
with their real life
Hammer horror stories!**

PETER THORNE

Football World

Published November 2004 by
Football World
Tel: (01708) 379 877

©Copyright Football World

All rights reserved.
Without limiting the rights under copyright reserved above,
no part of this publication may be reproduced, stored in or
introduced into a retrieval system, or, transmitted, in any
form or by any means (electronic, mechanical,
photocopying, recording or otherwise) without the prior
written permission of the copyright owner of this book.

Printed by Cox & Wyman Ltd, Reading, Berkshire

Distributed by Vine House Distribution Ltd
Waldenbury, North Common, Challey, East Sussex,
BN8 4DR, England.
Tel: (01825) 723398
Email: sales@vinehouseuk.co.uk

Set in Helvetica Roman

ISBN 0 9548336 2 7

To

Gail for breathing life
Natalie for putting flesh on the bones
Alex V for giving houseroom
Michael for keeping the faith

And

My Mum and Dad for everything else

Dedicated to the memory of my Grandfather,
Charles Wiggington – he warned me!

Acknowledgements

Thanks to Alex V for providing the foreword, allowing me to pollute his excellent site and also for his technical expertise.

Appreciation to Miss G and Home and Away who proofread my scrawl, corrected my poor grasp of punctuation and made suggestions – none of which were rude.

Thanks also to Henry Winter and the *Daily Telegraph* for allowing me to use quotes from their interview with Glenn Roeder.

A special acknowledgment to my best mate, Paul Nelson, who introduced me to the delights of Saturday afternoon on the terraces and taught me all the words to 'Tiptoe through the North Bank'.

Apologies to Natalie for not being able to use her great drawing after it has given me so much service over these past five years. Perhaps an update can be your next dissertation?

Fan comments in this book are taken from web site www.westhamonline.net and were posted online over the past few years in response to the Billy Blagg column. Many of these comments needed to be restored from archive and they were not always in an easily recognisable format. I have tried to keep posters' names and comments together where possible but apologise if any errors have been made in transcript.

No alterations have been made to the posts barring grammatical, legal and space-induced changes and these posts have been used to portray the fluctuating fortunes and beliefs of the fans at the time. There is no attempt to make anyone look ridiculous or show anybody in a poor light. I've managed that quite adequately myself, thanks!

Special thanks must go to the supporters of West Ham Online who constantly amuse, annoy and stimulate with their comments. This book would not have been possible without their input and so I would like to thank every contributor whose postings I have used. In order of appearance, you are credited below. Please don't seek me out for a drink, though – times are hard all round!

Special thanks to:
Gutted-hammer, Cygnet, Aiken Drum, Iron, alfs barnet, Norn Iron Andy, plw, Ged, Michael T, cOOL cOL, Russ of the BML, Nemesis, Bob the ball, Lady hammer, the medici popes, MATT, Dan L, sideshow Bob, twinhammer1, action, Mrs S, Easthammer, Natty Noo, jonthehammer, daveoflondon, Alex G, Carricks Pint, Grumpster, simon.s, Lee S, BMU, Rochford Hammer, West of London, Wiff, Tonka, Clarkie, Frankie, Swiss Toni, HR From Down Under, NorthBanker, Neilson, Nimods, Tim Johnson, Bill from Barnet, Goody-Ireland, North of Watford, Dirty from Chafford 100, Daren, Iain Dowie's Love Child, Martin, Down to bare bones, East side Eric, Rainham Pete, MikeyD, Petert, Upton Spark, Hammer Boy, Mr Egg, Saitchy, Ol BLue Eyes, Gerry, Adam L, Wattie, Nash, W.E, Saphron, Ginger Iron, Lady J, Dave, Paul d, Oscar, armchair, Knobby, Walky, GMAN, Mad Dog, Macca, Woody, GeoffT, Fizz, Steve, Ironman, Cardiff Irons, The Virus, Lukie, Nels, Miss G, Bill–Sydney Oz, Any Old Iron, AfM, Scuffler, Gerald Irons, Duncan, Jayee, PaulN, Reality Check, Whufcroe, The Vulture, jack flash, Kevin Isaac, Bignumbernine, Sanfranjef, FABIO, Telgee, Minty, Hotplates Davis, Flea Taxi, Anonny, SD, Cleatus, Dee Hammer, Dibersdownunder, Vhammer, Earl of Wakefielder, Tony the Driver, Rhysm, Fred, Peatburn, Upton Parker, KLM, Johnnie Boy, Onliner, AdamL, Johnnie Goat, RDM, Paolo, Clack, Baron von Evilswine, Mokum hammer, Dev, Sutton soul hammer, Davey B, Tony M, Blunders, Paulo Di Godio, D. Rollo, brownout, Martin Peters, Dutch Courage, Strong Dreams, Krap not Pu, philofacts, RIP, Manse, Tacchini kid, Thirsty, Midfield General, Beaklington, Mansfield, chang klan, Sandgroperhammer, Ozziehammer, Boxa, StR, JayeMPee, alfie romeo, DJ. Oscar, Mick the most, ironphilly, Rhyme, NAOMIM, Quest Jambonnier, Tynan, Wally, Pin-Up,

Confused Hammer, KIDDERS, AdelaideHammer, South
Sydney Hammer, Paddy Hammer, Frank White, Tibbsy,
WestHam Family, Bubblehead, Claret Hoop, Trevor
Brooking's Claret 'N' Blue Army, How Now Brown Cow,
Distraught Hammer, irisiris, HOK, highbury hammer, The iCe
CrEaM BoY, Alex x, inconsistant fc, selektah, mallard,
HAMMERDOWNUNDER, doomhunk, Eric Minnesota USA,
Tricky Dev, Kevin in Nova Scotia, Ronald_antly, dave,
Terminator 2, Johnny The Web, out now brown cow, Don
Watts, Steadmania, Captain _ Flashman, The Joker, Snailsy,
marky ironworks 1895, Senor Coconut, Aussie Mike, TCS,
Our Dave, Herts Hammer, The Prof, madhammerette,
Confused, Lowell, R Milne, Alvie, Joshua, GEEDEE, Dev,
Kezza, Claude Du Vall, cuzoftheeast, Saracen, Balto,
Wham1966, Essex Hammer, greenie1, Chickenrun, cOOL
cOL, whuami, norwaytips, X, GL, Couchy, Upton Park Mark,
Tim A, Si., Ashy, ff, sploosh, Bob the ball, MS in the West,
Alf Gandhi, North Bank Nelson, Withnail, Boyatthammer,
EastEndGeezer, angola, gianni, bubbleblower, Den Watts,
Morrissey, ONE IRON, Ali F, Hacko, Adray, Norwich hammer,
Claret&blueblood, RdUeSpSrEeLsLsed, HQ_Monaro, Sir Alf,
Melbourne hammer, snaggletooth, Woody, knob-chops,
Badhabit, Bullybaggio, keddy, Upton Park=Mecca,
Sxboy_66, mugabe, cd hammer, CaptainBlueAndClaret,
OhhhhMattyMatty!, North Banker, DavidL, BarrowBoy, FU
Chairman Brown, Herbie Hammer, Twist & Shout, Scribbler,
Bedford Rascal

Foreword

It's a pleasure to be asked to provide a foreword to this volume – Billy asked me for something upbeat and lively to set the tone for the rest of the book. And after finally managing to track me down through my therapist I was finally persuaded to jot down a few positive notes. Then, when the medication wore off, I tore them up and wrote these instead . . .

I note that studies of plane crash survivors indicate that those who recover best as a result of a tragedy are those who can more easily find hope in despair. Indeed, some people use such an event to refocus their lives and overcome prior problems using the tragedy as a springboard. This is known as the 'perceived benefit' concept, and, frankly, I'm amazed that the club don't hand out leaflets on the subject before every game, because it should be crucial education for the long-suffering West Ham fan.

There are also those for whom it's all too easy to become deeply cynical and wallow fruitlessly in despair . . . and it's in that spirit that westhamonline.net was born in 1997.

The first webpage began with a doctored photograph of Ian Bishop emerging from a toilet bowl, *Trainspotting*-style, and thus the standards were set for the next seven years. As a forum for lost voices wailing hopelessly in the darkness to each other it has been invaluable in mine and many others' personal therapy. One day many of us hope to recover to live normal, useful lives – until then the voices of Billy Blagg and his online Friends are a guiding light.

What the internet provides well (other than porn, obviously) is the equal platform it gives everyone to express an opinion. Whatever your age, background and standards of personal hygiene, you can have a voice. Without the invaluable online community at the website, I not only wouldn't enjoy being a West Ham fan so much, but also I would never have heard of the High Street Honeys or played an amusing web game where you have to bash a penguin along the ice with a baseball bat. The internet plays a vital social function for like-minded people, in that it keeps us off the streets at night.

With the advent of fanzines and now fan sites, the club and the media can't control the flow of information like they used to – the fans are now more clued up than ever before and can see through smokescreens and make up their own minds. It's at the stage now where many of the fans know more about the workings of their own club than the tabloid hacks and even many of the employees of the club themselves.

In short, the fans are more of a pain in the arse than ever before.

It's from this background that Billy Blagg was born – a warm-hearted keyboard warrior keeping us warm in the bitter nuclear winter that is West Ham's recent history. I fully expect him to become such a hot property that we'll expect the bigger London clubs to be putting in a bid. But westhamonline.net is not a selling website, we'll never get anywhere if we let writers like Billy Blagg go, I've been having sleepless nights over the transfer for weeks – just slip the brown envelope under the door...

I'm delighted, and not at all jealous, that Peter has put together such an informed, enjoyable and highly readable account of our club's demise. The title alone makes me shudder with fear at the prospect of Freddy Krueger lookalikes stalking the roads outside the ground – if you've seen the look of some of the fanzine sellers, you'll know exactly what I mean. And if you're anything like me you'll read the book experiencing the whole gamut of emotions – disappointment, anger, pain, anguish, regret, nausea, vomiting, hopelessness, religious despair, self-loathing, a cold bath. Alternatively, cut out the middle man and head straight to the off-licence.

I'd like to congratulate Peter, in particular, for writing the only book on modern British history that doesn't try to tie in every bloody thing with the advent of Tony Blair and Cool Brittania. I also agree with Peter's decision to remove the chapter linking the accelerating problem of global warming back to the ill-advised purchase of Titi Camara – the public just aren't ready for the truth.

At its heart, what the book really reminds us is that without some sense of hope we really have nothing. Yes, we have nothing. See you at the bar.

Alex V
October 2004

Contents

Introduction 1

1. Mannygate 6

2. We Are Not a Selling Club 21

3. Where's the Money Gone? 31

4. Los Glenndos 48

5. The Rocky Road Ahead 58

6. Down and Out 79

7. Caretaker Manager 95

8. Relegation is Such an Ugly Word 110

9. Managerial Merry-Go-Round 129

10. WHISTLE Down the Wind 155

11. The Play-Offs 166

12. Back on the Glory Trail 197

13. The Blaggers Crystal Balls 210

Introduction

I've never believed that football is more important than life and death. Nor do I think that the great Bill Shankly, the man credited with everyone's favourite football sound bite, ever really believed that either. You only have to watch the ten o'clock news to understand that football – even at its best – is nothing more than a magnificent irrelevance.

What I do think that football does, though, is hold a mirror to life itself. In much the same way as we suffer a multitude of emotions as we walk life's rocky road, so we experience similar feelings over a 90-minute match or a full football season.

Excitement, pleasure, humour, joy and an enormous sense of well-being are all yours – if you support Arsenal. If you're a West Ham supporter, however, you can expect a hefty dose of cold reality. Disappointment, agony, anger, frustration, disappointment (and that's not a typo either – the Hammers provide you with a second dose) are all good friends of the average claret and blue fan.

But all those emotions have to be channelled somewhere, and that is why I believe that West Ham fans are second to none in the support of their beloved team. Being a Hammers' fan means being in touch with life's hardships. Together we are all keenly aware that the grass isn't greener over the hill; the glass is most definitely half-empty; and the sky might be blue today but it will certainly pee with rain by the end of the week. In much the same way that those who suffer personal hardship seem to appreciate life's golden moments better, then so can a West Ham supporter look at a Man U fan crying – because his team have been pipped to the Premiership title by a single point in the last match of the season – and see that 'disaster' for what it is.

Apart from the birth of my children and a few other personal moments, West Ham United has provided me with some of my favourite memories. Fortunately, I'm old enough to remember trophies won and England's finest players parading their skills with the crossed hammers on their chests; it's not all been gloom and despondency. But even when things went against us – and how long have you got? – there has been a fantastic sense of camaraderie and gallows humour ever-present in supporting West Ham.

Examples? Well, a 6-0 League Cup semi-final defeat on a plastic pitch in rain-sodden Oldham springs to mind; where the rain running down my face mingled with the blood from a large cut on my forehead, obtained via an ill-judged lob of a full beer can on the coach journey up. Then there's the FA Cup semi-final defeat against Nottingham Forest where the Forest fans could only watch and wonder at the joyous support given to a team 4-0 down. Then there was the Heysel stadium in Brussels in '76; the monsoon on the Stretford End watching Bobby Moore save a penalty after he'd replaced a concussed Bobby Ferguson in goal; being used for brick-related target practice at Hull and Port Vale. Hell, I'm starting to get all emotional here.

I used to have a cartoon pinned to my office wall. It depicted two women walking behind a Neanderthal-looking man: "So is he passionate?" one woman asked. "Passionate? Yeah, I'll say," replied the other. "Just let anyone start to criticise West Ham!" It seemed to sum up the average Hammers fan to me. Just like our theme song, fortune always did seem to be hiding, we had dreams but they would fade and die. All we had was our passion, humour and – if we were fortunate – our memories.

I'll never forget the day, in April 1997, that I first took my children to a match at Upton Park. I was grateful my daughter wanted to go; I didn't expect her to keep the attendance up (ultimately she didn't) but she was at that touching age where she wanted to do what her Dad did. My son, on the other hand, I hoped would keep the faith while not necessarily reaching the lunacy level that his father had adopted (which has pretty much been the case).

Resplendent in new mini replica kits, scarves and hats, they excitedly soaked up the pre-match atmosphere and waited for the start of the great adventure. The match in question was against Everton and for the first time ever I took some seats in the Family Enclosure. I noted the fathers with their children and got talking to one bloke in front of me who, like me, had brought his son for the first time. We talked proudly in that insane way that only football fans can muster as we spoke of our hopes for the future and the way we had somehow enriched our children's lives by introducing them to the joys of their local team. Not for them some obscure support of a team that played in a part of the country in which they didn't live. This was *their* team; a bond forged over decades and handed down to me by my Grandfather who forbade me to put a picture of Tottenham Hotspur on my wall when I was four because it 'wasn't right'. This was a birthright, a family heirloom.

The game began well with West Ham fully in control; we went 2-0 up thanks to two Paul Kitson goals. Just after half time we were awarded a penalty, which John Hartson would normally have taken. But he offered the kick to Kitson who, instead of completing his hat trick, failed to connect properly and the keeper saved. Nevertheless, a two goal lead looked good value on the balance of play.

But – and this book is about West Ham United so there will be loads of 'buts' – it didn't last. An hour into the match Everton pulled a goal back and, with West Ham furiously back-pedalling, the equaliser came 10 minutes before the end. In fact, only a fine Shaka Hislop save prevented the ignominy of a home defeat.

The sense of disappointment was palpable. My kids, who had celebrated the Hammers' goals in true style, turned to me as the equaliser went in with a questioning type of "this isn't supposed to happen is it, Dad?" look. I groaned and held my head in my hands and I looked up just in time to see the other father glance over at me. He said nothing. Neither did I but our eyes met and a message passed briefly between us. That message was: 'This is it, kids. This is the way of West Ham. You won't like it, and you'll never ever get used to it, but accept it because it's your burden'.

This book is about that burden. Seen through the eyes of a cast of players from the West Ham website, *www.westhamonline.net*, it charts the astonishing decline of one of the best young squad of players ever to assemble outside the environs of Old Trafford. The main threads of this book were taken from the Billy Blagg column posted on the West Ham Online site at the time the events occurred (those in normal plain text). The fan comments were posted at the same time, giving supporters the chance to respond to Blagg's views while expressing their own.

The only changes made to the original postings have been grammatical, legal or as clarification. Original thoughts expressed at the time have not been changed.

This was not a book written with the benefit of hindsight – in many ways this has given a better perspective on events. For example, it's very hard to imagine now that when Harry Redknapp was sacked, I was sceptical that the vacant position should be offered to Alan Curbishley. At the time, West Ham looked to have a bright future with a crop of young stars most clubs would have given their Quality Hotels for, while Charlton Athletic were Premiership wannabes with little chance of survival. It seemed to me then that nothing was to be gained by reverting to type and re-introducing a Hammers old boy into a club destined to march boldly into the future.

Changing the thoughts and feelings that were prevalent to me at the time may have made me look better, and possibly have got me a job on the Lottery Draw on Saturday nights, but the real essence of the book would then have been lost. Because this is a book about what it is to be a fan with all its knee-jerk reactions, contradictions and untruths. It's about having a set of heroes one week and a gaggle of buffoons the next. It's about yesterday's heroes and today's false idols.

It's also the story of what should, and could, have been. It's a tale of ineptitude and embarrassment, of poor decisions and strange goings on. It's about a team that should have entered the new Millennium at a peak but it's also about a club that continually gets it wrong.

For there could just as well be another book on the poor

decisions that allowed the 1986 West Ham team, that challenged for the league title until the last day of the season before finishing third, to disintegrate without a fight. It could be about the glorious mid-60s team that ruled Europe and had three World Cup winners in it but floundered in the league for want of investment and insistence on doing things the 'proper way'. Or it could be about the 1975-76 Cup-winning and European final side that was stuff-full of England under-23 players who were suddenly all has-beens before they were 25.

In short, it's about a dream that continually fades and dies. It's about disappointment and anger – sure! - but it's also about humour, a sense of belonging and a community spirit that is second to none. Ultimately, it may be pain but it's *our* pain.

This is the way of West Ham United. Read it and weep.

Chapter 1

MANNYGATE
December 1999

West Ham United had begun the 90s in a poor state. For the first time in nearly three decades they had been reduced to a purely journeyman team desperately searching for an identity. A working example of a yo-yo side, they bounced from First Division to Second Division before the Football Association took pity on them and renamed the First Division to the Premiership, thereby enabling the Hammers to be relegated and stay in the same division at the same time. A masterstroke!

In 1994, first team coach Harry Redknapp took over the managerial reins from Billy Bonds in a coup that means neither man speaks to the other to this day. Bonds was a legendary player and captain but his managerial reign was viewed as partial failure because, despite gaining promotion under his leadership, the Hammers seemed unable to hold on to top flight status.

In fact, during his tenure, Bonds had had to steer the club through the mire of the ill-fated Bond Scheme, whereby the West Ham United board had attempted to get the fans to raise the finance to help build the new all-seater stadia demanded by the Taylor Report following the Hillsborough tragedy of 1989. The fans had fought the board on the issue and West Ham went through a traumatic period that affected the club at every level. 'Bonzo' seemed disillusioned by the political manoeuvring during this period and his leadership seemed to lack substance, unusual in view of his legendary buccaneering captaincy and playing style.

The West Ham board must have felt similarly as they attempted to move Bonds 'upstairs' to a figurehead capacity while promoting his assistant, Redknapp, to the manager's role. Bonds was unhappy with the proposed move and left the club, allowing Redknapp to take full control of team affairs.

Redknapp started his period as manager in the style that soon became his own. Running the club in much the same way as a used car salesman would run his showroom, Our 'Arry wheeled and dealed as he bought and sold with impunity, gathering around him a succession of cheap deals, rejects, foreign imports, rusty buckets and sporty classics some of which paid off while others didn't.

However, while all this was going on Redknapp was apparently working a miracle behind the scenes, completely overhauling the club's youth policy in the knowledge that it would be lifeblood to a club seemingly always struggling to hold its own. Despite several close shaves over the years, by 1999, things seemed to be paying dividends. Redknapp's skill in finding a cheap deal began to meld with the burgeoning youth policy. Frank Lampard Jnr and Rio Ferdinand, players destined to play for their country virtually from the moment they pulled on a Hammers second XI shirt, were already ever-present in the first team. Redknapp had turned an Italian genius named Paolo Di Canio from an unwanted football nomad into a genuine Cockney hero. Everywhere you went there was talk of the outstanding crop of youngsters to be found in the youth team. When a young Joe Cole led the side to a 9-0 aggregate FA Youth Cup final victory over Coventry City in 1999, in front of a massive Upton Park crowd, there was a real sense of anticipation in the East End air.

After finishing fifth in the 1998-99 season, West Ham were invited to take part in a tin-pot pre-season tournament called the Intertoto Cup (or the Inter-Dorothy as one WHO poster called it). Victory in this would ensure a place in that season's UEFA Cup. The Hammers not only won but also pulled off a superb victory at Metz in the second leg of the Intertoto final after losing 1-0 in the first leg at Upton Park.

Our European tour didn't last long, though. Lessons needed to be learnt on how to play away legs in Europe but, even so, there was strong anticipation of another European place via a high league placing, or by that perennial favourite, the cup final appearance.

By December 1999, after a brisk start in the league thanks mainly to the Hammers' early season start in the Intertoto, West Ham's momentum had slowed somewhat. They occupied a mid-table place and had suffered an embarrassing defeat at the hands of Tranmere Rovers in the FA Cup. Just three days after that defeat, however, they made amends at Upton Park by beating Aston Villa on penalties in a pulsating Worthington Cup quarter-final. The fans eagerly anticipated Christmas and the prospect of a two-legged semi-final tie against Leicester City early in the New Year. And then came the astonishing news...

In the 113th minute of the tie against Villa, Redknapp had sent on a young reserve winger, mainly to waste a bit of time and help keep possession. That player was Manny Omoyinmi and his name was to become forever linked to the club's unerring ability to shoot itself in the foot.

Omoyinmi had been on loan to Gillingham earlier in the season and, apparently unknown to West Ham, had played for the Gills in an earlier round of the Worthington Cup, thus making himself ineligible to play for Hammers in the same competition that season. His appearance in the claret and blue (as sub for Paulo Wanchope) meant they had fielded an ineligible player and, despite the fact Omoyinmi had barely touched the ball in his seven-minute appearance, West Ham were ordered to replay the game.

The nightmare was about to begin...

BLAGG, Dec 1999

I couldn't sleep on Saturday night. I kept waking up and thinking "what a strange dream". I kept dreaming that West Ham were being thrown out of the Worthington Cup for fielding an ineligible player and hoped, rather like those dreams where you're falling out of an aeroplane or a crazed dentist has removed all your teeth, that I would wake up, find I was on terra firma with my teeth still intact, sigh serenely and return to sleep. Not Saturday though. No, not on Saturday.

I can't believe the club has done it to us again. I can't believe that I am more upset and angry than I was after the FA Cup debacle against Tranmere. I said then that, whatever happened, the team must not hide behind the Aston Villa result and I stand by that. But, as ever with West Ham, the manner of the win over Villa did cloud the insipid Tranmere performance. The excitement and drama of the defeat of Villa should have stayed with us all the way to Wembley. Now they are to be erased from the memory, just like the result will be erased from the record books.

I know you are all asking this but HOW THE **** CAN THIS HAPPEN? I was going to demand the head of the perpetrator on a plate but I see in the morning paper that Harry accepts full responsibility and I'm not sure I want H to go. But is H right to accept responsibility? Is he not just getting all Roosevelt on us and doing the honourable thing?

You see, what I can't accept is Omoyinmi's part in this. Why didn't the stupid **** say something! I read one comment in the paper that said: 'He's only a young lad – he probably thought it was all right'. How young exactly is Manny, then? Five? Do you know, I'm even starting to blame myself for this? I should have known that he played for Gillingham in an earlier round and telephoned West Ham to tell them. That's how stupid and embarrassed I feel about the whole thing.

Earlier this year we all bridled when Eyal Berkovic left the club with the parting shot that described us as a 'pub team'. Now I'm scared in case Rio's mum forgets to wash the shirts and they have to play in 'skins' on Boxing Day.

What a stupid, stupid mistake, West Ham! After our FA Cup defeat last week, I told you to hold your heads in shame. This week I reckon I ought to send a box of Band-Aid plasters to the club for Christmas so that they can all place them on their faces to hide the ugly scars that will result from having to drag their chins along the road – because that's how low the heads should go this week. On Wednesday night we had the look of a team with its name on the Cup? Not now!

What galls nearly as much as the club's incompetence, though, is that horrible feeling that we have been sold down the river by the Football League. Had Man U or Arsenal made the same mistake – not that they would, of course – would they have been ordered to replay? I thought the Villa board made themselves look ridiculous with their bluster and posturing over the Omoyinmi appearance. Frankly, I can't remember him touching the ball twice, so I think they made a lot of their demands. They lost fair and square and the lad hardly made a difference to the result. I suspect that had Villa fielded an ineligible player in identical circumstances, then West Ham would not have demanded a replay in view of the minimal effect of the player in the short time he was on. In fact, I think the club demanding a replay at all may have faintly embarrassed me.

Nevertheless, The League has to be seen to be doing the right thing and a re-match is the result. We only have ourselves to blame (notice how I'm taking responsibility now?). But how bad do you feel about this? And don't you think that, yet again, greater forces are at work? I haven't been this low since we were relegated in 1978.

Still, it's not all doom and gloom, is it? The League was good enough not to throw us out but just demand a replay. They even let us re-play it at home. So we'll win in January and the march will be on again, won't it?

I think we all know the answer to that now, don't we…

Gutted-hammer
Noooooooooooooooooooooooooooooooooooooooooooooo…

Cygnet
As soon as I heard the decision to replay the tie, I rang up Radio Five Live's *6-0-6* to point out that Villa manager John Gregory, who is serving a touchline ban, came on to the pitch twice (full time and extra-time) to coach the players and he had far more impact than our substitute who touched the ball twice. Ultimately futile, I know, but it made me feel better…

Aiken Drum
Got a call this morning from my mate telling me it's looking like a replay and I thought it was a wind up – can't believe it's true.

******* typical!

ONLY West Ham could do this – how the hell can we not realise he was cup-tied? How the hell did HE not realise he was cup-tied? You just know we're going to lose the replay – you just know it.

Iron

Can't believe it at all.

Same old West Ham, taking the piss!

The game itself was memorable for the fact that we went 2-1 down in injury time, only for Paolo to score a (dubious!) penalty in the 93rd minute. Then Southgate missed his spot kick in the penalty shoot-out. Oh, how we laughed!

The worst part was that Manny only played for about seven or eight minutes and touched the ball about twice!

Why did we bring him on in the first place? It may turn out to be one of the most expensive and worst substitutions in history.

alfs barnet

Typical West Ham, couldn't organise a piss up in a brewery. If I see Harry's sheepish face on the telly one more time, blaming the player, I am going to throw my West Ham coffee mug through the screen.

Norn Iron Andy

My over-riding thoughts are, 'only at West Ham'.

Only at West Ham would you bring on a useless short-arse with six minutes to go.

Only at West Ham would that useless short-arse manage to avoid touching the ball in that six minute period, but still manage to decide the outcome of the game

Only at West Ham would that useless short-arse have managed to play for someone else in the competition without anyone bothering to check or stop it at the time.

plw

I can't believe that so many people could not notice that Manny had played already in the Cup, Harry, Mackerel (sic), Manny himself. I couldn't slag Villa for using it to their advantage, though – we would've done the same thing.

Ged

How can a manager bring a player back from loan, not check such details and then blame the player?

Sure, perhaps the player should have piped up, but I'd be surprised if many (pardon the pun) players are entirely familiar with the FA's rules regarding the administration of such competitions.

It beggars belief.

Michael T

Don't the club the player has been loaned to have to get permission to cup-tie the player? Surely they just can't play him if they fancy? So someone at West Ham must have said it was OK to play him in a previous round. What a balls-up!

cOOL cOL

That ***** Mackerel (sic) should be sacked. How can anyone make a mistake as huge as this?

I bet the greedy bastards don't reduce the ticket prices for the replay either.

Russ of the BML

Didn't the dopey *********** know he'd already played in this tournament? Tsk, send him home to Gillingham!

Nemesis

My mate has a half share in a season ticket at Gillingham and had seen the League Cup game in question.

So what did he do? Did he realise Manny was on the bench, and what this could mean? Did he contact a steward, so word could quietly be passed to Redknapp?

Or did he turn to me as we were leaving and say: "Oh God, I saw him play at Priestfield!"

Bob the ball

It should be obvious that the player is to blame. He knows exactly in what competition he's previously played. He may be stupid but where football matches are concerned, trust me, the bloke knew he had already played in the competition. Like Harry, I just could not believe the stupidity of the player, and the lack of checking done by the club's player registration secretary, who has ultimate responsibility for such things. Of course it's much easier to blame Redknapp

Lady hammer

Why is the player to blame? I mean, when you have an important Cup game coming up and you have just bought a player back from a loan period, is it not the first thing you find out? Jeez!

the medici popes

Why would Manny know what competitions he played in? He just turns up and plays.

Administrators administrate. Players play.

The playing staff of both clubs are without blame. The administrators of both clubs are culpable of a terrible lack of care. We may never know what went on in the lead-up to Manny being made available. My guess is no one really checked. Maybe Redknapp's squad sheet never got to GM's office in time to run a check, who knows? No one lied – it was a **** up. (With a slight sigh of resignation) . . . How awfully West Ham.

Southgate's boots: Adidas crowd-finders?

MATT

Surely only West Ham, out of all the 90-odd clubs in the leagues, could be capable of such incompetence. I laughed at first, but soon stopped when it began to sink in. I just know that we'll **** it up this time, and lose the replay.

By the way, I believe it's Redknapp's ultimate responsibility. If a manager has a player on loan at his club, and wants to play him in a Cup game, then he must contact the manager he's borrowed him from to get his permission. This is an obvious rule to have, because his club may have plans to play him later in the competition. Redknapp must have OK'd it in the first place, so he should have remembered, eh?

To turn around and blame it on a young player, who may or may not be up to speed on the rules, is cowardly and unprofessional.

Dan L

I got into work to an email from a Spurs colleague saying: "I'm not even going to type it because you won't believe me but safe to say your two-bit club has club has raised the bar this time".

A couple of phone calls later confirmed the bloke as spot on.

We sacked him yesterday – serves him right!

It won't tarnish one of my best-ever West Ham memories, though. All the Villa players were getting the usual boos coming up to take their kicks but when Southgate approached the stand, we all clapped and cheered. When he missed, I couldn't cheer for laughing. Priceless.

sideshow Bob

A lot of us are blaming Gillingham, who (according to Redknapp) told WH that he HAD NOT played. Why did they say that?

twinhammer1

Absolute gross incompetence, totally incomprehensible.

action

Blaming Omoyinmi is absolutely scandalous. Redknapp should take the rap, as he should know which players he's loaning out and how they're getting on.

It's also Redknapp's fault for making the substitution. The only reason he subbed Wanchope was to avoid having to tell him that he didn't want him to take a penalty. Do you really think Omoyinmi was brought on:

a) to win us the game in the last few minutes?
b) because he's a penalty specialist?

Redknapp should go.

Mrs S

I just can't believe it. How could a player not know that he had already played in the competition? He must have known the rules – even I know, and I'm a female!

Harry allegedly asked him if he had played and he said 'No'.

The club phoned Gillingham to ask and they said 'No'.

So who is to blame?

In my eyes, the player. He knew he had played yet he desperately wanted to play for us and, I expect, thought no one would notice.

Easthammer

I'm sorry but this doesn't make any sense.

You say Harry asked the player?

"Excuse me, Manny, but I may put you on this evening, you're not Cup-tied are you?"

You say WHU phoned Gillingham?

"Excuse me, but you had one of our players on loan a few weeks back – can't remember if he played any games for you at all, can you?"

Manny knew he had played but decided to keep quiet?

"I know, I'll slip on in extra time – I'm sure no-one will notice".

That can't really happen in a multi-million pound business surely?

None of this makes any sense whatsoever. I'm not having a go at anyone in particular but some of these Manny said/Harry asked/Gills told us stories must be pure speculation. Will we ever find out? What do you think?

DLAQQ, today

As the arguments continued over who was responsible for the error, an unseemly squabble broke out as Harry Redknapp appeared to accuse Manny Omoyinmi who, not unreasonably, shrunk from the media spotlight as he suddenly found himself thrust onto the back pages for reasons he could never have dreamed of.

Many inevitably asked why Redknapp himself wasn't aware of where and when his own players were, if there was a danger of them becoming Cup-tied.

However, it soon became clear that it was unlikely that player or manager would be sacked and the fickle finger of fate inevitably turned onto the club administration team, particularly ex-Sheffield Wednesday secretary Graham Mackrell.

What made the issue worse was that West Ham had rather surprisingly dispensed with the services of popular managing director Peter Storrie a few months earlier. Storrie had been largely responsible for raising the profile of the club in the latter years of Redknapp's reign and he and Harry had appeared to be working well in unison, with Storrie himself then becoming the mouthpiece for the club.

An avuncular and approachable character, Storrie seemed, in the eyes of many, to be one of the good guys and his dismissal raised eyebrows as to whom he might have upset – chairman Terry Brown or manager H?

Whatever, West Ham had replaced Storrie with Graham Mackrell, a much respected secretary who had previously worked for the Hillsborough outfit and it was Mackrell who was now in the spotlight.

Amusingly, so high was Storrie's profile with the club compared to that of Mackrell, that, even today, many people blame Storrie for 'Mannygate', wrongly assuming he was still at the club at the time of the fiasco.

Meanwhile, in January 2000, the replay against Aston Villa took place and gave us a good opportunity to look at the madness that inflicts even the most sensible football supporter.

The club reissued tickets as per the original game, ensuring that everybody sat in exactly the same place in the ground with exactly the same supporters around them. The fans responded in kind.

Inevitably, the writing was writ large on the wall and despite taking the lead, the Hammers fell behind in extra-time before being awarded a penalty that Paolo Di Canio failed to convert (David James saved). Another late strike meant the result went against the Hammers, 3-1, and Aston Villa went through in a quarter-final tie they had already lost.

BLAGG, Jan 2000

How insane can one person become when faced with replaying a game we had already won in December? In order to recreate the same result as the original game, I decided to do everything exactly as I had done in the first match.

I left work at the same time, had the same tea, wore the same clothes (even though it was much warmer weather than when the original game was played in December), travelled the same route to the ground, parked in the same place outside my Mother and Father's, popped in to see them as before and even refused a much needed drink as I hadn't had one prior to the first game. I then walked the same way from East Ham to the Boleyn and took my same seat in the Bobby Upper.

Once inside the ground, I saw the same faces that I had seen in December. We chatted, I asked them if they had had a good Christmas and, feeling among friends, I admitted to my lunatic ritual. Guess what? I was not alone. The bloke next to me had gone to the same pub, for the same drink and ensured that he entered through the same door – even though it was easier to go in another way.

Another fan, much to the consternation of his wife, had fished out the same underpants from the washing basket – even though they were due a wash.

All around me everyone had made attempts to recreate the original setting. How we laughed.

Amusing though all this was, there was still something bothering me. You see, I had made an unfortunate mistake during the build-up because I had dropped the ticket for my best mate round his house on Sunday and, consequently, met him *inside* the ground instead of outside at the usual spot. So was it my fault we lost?

Ultimately, Tuesday night was too awful to contemplate and I really can't get my head around the fact that the semi-final place has been taken from us. I put no blame on the team. We didn't play badly and could just as easily have won. But, let's be honest, we knew it was going to happen. Nobody wanted to commit the sacrilege of saying it, although I hinted at it in a previous column, but there was no way West Ham were going to win any rematch and Ian Taylor's two goals, when he shouldn't have even been on the pitch after his two tackles on Di Canio and Cole in the first game, were proof of it.

At times, I almost expected a giant hand to come down from the sky and flick any goal-bound shot away like some intergalactic Subbuteo game. I'm not a particularly religious man but watching West Ham sometimes makes me feel that greater forces are at work and, believe me, the Big Referee in the Sky must be a Tottenham supporter.

I don't really feel like doing anything now other than going on a long holiday until next August but I feel duty bound to add some type of underline to recent events. Some of what I have to say may sound harsh. Some may contradict previously held views but – and make no mistake about it – a major issue has arisen here with Tranmere and Mannygate. It's similar to a company, previously chugging along quite comfortably, suddenly losing a million pounds; or a transport system, usually safe, suddenly having a few serious accidents; or a marriage, happy for many years, suddenly teetering with the husband coming home late reeking of perfume. I think I've strained my point. So here goes.

Firstly, a rematch was a travesty. West Ham was incompetent and stupid but the punishment in no way fitted the crime. In an FA Cup game last weekend, Sunderland lost a match to Tranmere even though the Scousers inadvertently had 12 men on the pitch for several minutes. Compare Sunderland's reaction at Prenton Park with those of Doug Ellis after the 'Mannygate' incident. Villa should be ashamed of their reprieve and I hope that Leicester turn them over in the semis. At least that way, Tony Cottee will earn the chance of gaining a well-deserved medal.

Secondly, Manny Omoyinmi must never pull on a claret and blue shirt again. Look at how much that young man earns a week and look at the opportunities afforded if he makes a leap back to Premiership status. Look at the lifestyle of Jamie Redknapp, David Beckham or, even, Rio Ferdinand. Now look at your own pay packet. Can you remember where you were working three months ago? Of course you can!

Omoyinmi has no defence and his pathetic silence says more about him than anything. Offload the idiot and insert a clause in his next contract that says we take a big piece of the pie if he ever does get sold on for millions. Take no notice of nonsensical articles like those in the *Daily Mail* recently, accusing us of wanting a biblical 'eye for an eye' without 'turning the other cheek'. This is utter bollocks. This man is so stupid that he should be stripped of all his football wear and be forced to stack shelves in Iceland for the rest of his natural. There are people working in there with twice his IQ. That's Iceland, the store, by the way, not the country – although on second thoughts…

Similarly, I want no reprieve for Graham Mackrell or any secretary involved. Get them out, too.

Next, there must be serious questions asked about Manager H and Frank Lampard Snr. I appreciate the fact that West Ham was in a state when H was promoted to manager and he has built the club up to compete in Europe with a fine youth policy, but that says more about previous administrations than anything else.

This is a big club with a big catchment area of East London and Essex. We want more. Both men must be given warning. I want European qualification or a trophy by next season or serious questions must be answered. I'm sorry – but I've had enough. This isn't a 'sack the manager' knee-jerk reaction to an unwarranted cup defeat. Well, OK, perhaps it is. But I'm upset and I don't care.

Gutted-hammer
Nooooooooooooooooooooooooooooooooooooooooooooooo…

Norn Iron Andy
"Only at West Ham" could we contrive to lose the replay in the most heart-crushing way

Natty Noo
Out of a tie wo've already won! How do you all feel today? The repercussions from this will be far-reaching.

BLAGG, today
The club was hamstrung by the Villa result and eventually finished ninth in the final table. The reverberations continued for some time with disturbing finger-pointing by manager, player and administration staff. There was a general feeling that someone's head had to roll for the debacle and, rather inevitably, it turned out to be the dual heads of Club Secretary Graham Mackrell and Football Secretary Alison Dowd, who eventually took the brunt of the blame and both resigned.

On the announcement, chairman Terence Brown was quoted as saying: "The board would like to thank Mr Mackrell for all his hard work on behalf of the club since his appointment in June. We feel Graham has made an honourable decision but it seems a high price to have to pay for what was a small and genuine administrative error."

Mackrell himself said: "Whatever happens I'm responsible for administration here at West Ham United. The buck does stop with me. I felt it was the honourable thing to do to tender my resignation."

It may have been a genuine error – but small?

Manny Omoyinmi was last seen playing for National Conference side Gravesend (five goals from nine games at the time of writing). An excellent prospect at youth level, in retrospect, it's hard to figure who suffered more. Aston Villa lost the semi-final to Leicester City, enabling the Foxes to lift the Worthington Cup and Tony Cottee to get a well-deserved winners' medal.

I'm still waiting for the day, on Question of Sport, when Sue Barker asks: 'Who reached the semi-final of the Worthington Cup after going out in the quarter-final?'

Chapter 2

WE ARE NOT A SELLING CLUB
November 2000

West Ham approached the season following Mannygate with some trepidation. Although on paper the squad looked strong enough to challenge for a European place via the league and make a strong bid in the Cups, there was concern about the number of rumours linking the Hammers' star young players to top clubs already in Europe. The strong feeling was that West Ham needed to put itself into European contention in the 2000-01 season to ensure they held onto their 'crown jewels'.

After a slow start the Hammers were looking at a top six place as they entered the autumn schedule. Then, in November 2000, following months of speculation and denials from the club, it was announced that they had accepted an £18-million offer from Leeds United for England International Rio Ferdinand. This followed an impressive display from the centre-back in a rare 1-0 Hammers win at Elland Road just a few days previously. We may have been better off had we lost there 5-0 as usual.

BLAGG, Nov 2000

There are, so it is said, three types of lie. Lies, damned lies and statistics. But this in itself is also an untruth because there are actually four types of lies. Lies, damned lies, statistics . . . and quotes from football clubs.

It has long been a standing joke in football that if a chairman gives his manager a vote of confidence, then said manager is soon to be sacked. But that is really just the tip of a Titanic-sinking iceberg. How about these chestnuts: "He is not for sale at any price?" "I am trying to build a club here not destroy one?" or the classic "If I let my best players go, what message does that send out to the remaining ones?"

I'll put my cards on the table straight away and say that I felt physically sick when I read that the board had accepted an offer from Leeds for Rio Ferdinand. I write this with my hand shaking, barely able to contain my anger. I feel like crying. Would anyone at the *Daily Mail* or *Radio Five* understand this feeling? I doubt it. I'm only a fan and, traditionally, what we want for our clubs has nothing to do with reality. Strange really, isn't it? Without us no players would get paid, no stadiums would be filled and no TV sports coverage would be watched. But when it comes down to situations like an 18 million pounds bid for one of our own – hey, why worry? We can always get in someone from the Cameroon!

Although the above quotes are probably attributable to Harry, let me say straight away that I blame none of this week's debacle on the manager or Rio – although some support from one and some loyalty from the other wouldn't have gone amiss. H would obviously have loved to have kept Ferdinand and have some money although, for me, he is toeing the party line a little more strongly than I would like. Nevertheless, when Harry or someone says "that player is not available at any price", what he actually means is "that player is available but for a few million quid more than you are offering, matey".

In fact, it's probably worse than that. What H should say is: "I haven't the foggiest notion if that player is available – ask the bloody chairman!"

For, make no mistake, selling Rio Ferdinand is down to the board – and that makes West Ham a selling club and everybody knows it. The ink was barely dry on Wednesday's 'Paper we all love to hate' *Daily Mail* before the next edition proudly proclaimed that Chelsea had offered £8-million for Frederic Kanouté and the Blues were likely to get him as –

you've guessed it – WHU have a history of selling their prize assets. It doesn't take a genius to realise that Joe Cole, Frank Lampard and Michael Carrick, and anyone else who comes through our ranks over the next five years or so, will be moving on as a result of Rio's transfer. Cole and Lampard possibly for fees that makes Rio's look like mere bagatelle.

But going they will – as Yoda once said. Take no notice if Harry says otherwise this week – and he will – because it's got nothing to do with what H says or does.

What also galls me is the fact that my old nemesis, Pini Zahavi, has been quoted as saying: "Leeds are a fantastic club". No, they are f****** well not! Leeds have done well over the past few seasons and, historically, they had a good team in the 70s (I'm sorry, no team managed by Don Revie can ever be classed as great), but I don't think that this can be seen as anything other than a sideways move.

If someone wants to make some link between the Yorkshire club and WHU, then what they should really be looking at is the Leeds 1991-92 Championship-winning side. That team slogged its way to a trophy with such 'stars' as Lee Chapman, David Batty and Tony Dorigo supporting the undoubted talents of Cantona and Strachan, proving that you don't have to sport a multi-million pound outfit full of foreign players with silky ball skills to get you a Premiership trophy (are you listening too, Chelsea?). You can do it with some skilful players, some seasoned veterans and some emerging youngsters. Sound like any team you know?

In short, like Yosser Hughes, West Ham should look at that Leeds side and say: 'We're better than that' and 'I can do that!'

"We're not Arsenal or Manchester United", said Harry this week. No, we are not. But, how about remembering who we are rather than bothering about who we are not? Anyway – and I hate to be pedantic here – Rio hasn't been offered a chance to join either of the Red teams. He's off to join another team at the same level as us. Or at least, they would be at the same level if we didn't keep selling them our best players.

When Bobby Moore captained our side the top teams were known as the 'Big Five'. Manchester United (then big but not necessarily successful), Arsenal (always big and successful), Liverpool (once huge but slipped a bit in recent years), Everton (stop laughing at the back there!) and Spurs (Oh, all right then . . . hahahahhahahahah). So these teams always won the League, did they? Certainly not. Such giants of the game as Derby County and Nottingham Forest also managed it while Watford, QPR and Southampton came very close. Why? How? Simple! They had the best players and the best teams for a few seasons. And that could be us, too.

I said at the start of the season that we could go a long way if only we believed in ourselves. But the board doesn't seem to believe in West Ham and, consequently, neither do the manager, players or fans.

Surely, though, the biggest lie of all is "the transfer system may be ending soon and our best players could walk for nothing". Of course they could but that applies to everyone. On that day, if and when it comes, we would have as much chance as signing any player as any other Premiership club. It will be just down to what we can offer a prospective employee. If we look like we mean business, then they may be tempted. If we behave like a selling club, just ready to grab the cash, then we will deserve what we get.

Anyway, this lie looks even more preposterous when we view the fact that Harry intends to spend the Rio money on Rigobert Song and Titi Camara from Liverpool. Being as the "transfer system may be ending soon", why not wait until the Liverpool pair become free agents? At the moment, West Ham will be buying into the transfer system they predict is collapsing. It's crazy and it's also a lie!

The West Ham board are not accepting £18m for Rio because they might one day get nothing for him. They would take £18m regardless, because they are small-minded and can't see beyond the end of their next bank balance.

West Ham fans have been sold down the river this week by board and manager. I'm disgusted that Ferdinand has been sold to Leeds and I sadly predict that this is going to send a bad message to players still on our books.

What do you think Frank Jnr is thinking today? Had he progressed to Barcelona, Read Madrid or Lazio then I would have shook Rio's hand and wished him good luck. But moving up North is a kick in the teeth that none of us deserve. How will you feel when Peter Ridsdale parades our player before the Leeds fans on Sunday?

I don't care who Harry signs with the cash he has been handed. But make no mistake about it – nothing short of a Cup win or a European place will make amends for me. I wanted to see Ferdinand, Cole and Carrick parading a trophy in claret and blue but then who gives a flying one about what I wanted?

I'm only a fan and nobody has offered £18m for me to support Leeds!

action

i. You NEVER sell your home-grown talent. It demonstrates a complete lack of ambition. All the other young players will realise the club has no loyalty to them and will therefore demonstrate no loyalty in return – in short, all of the youth team players will leave as soon as a decent offer comes in.

ii. Rio Ferdinand is worth more than £18m to us. Look at the statistics of our defensive record whenever he's been injured. In short, we cannot defend. However, he has gone stale (see points below) over the last 12 months.

iii. Redknapp will be like a kid in a candy store with the money and all the other Premiership clubs will know we have cash to spend. Redknapp is also widely regarded within football as a joke manager and therefore will be unable to attract players of any repute to the club.

iv. If the club had any ambition they would not sell Rio but move Redknapp on and get in a top quality manager instead. This will demonstrate to players like Rio that they can move their careers on with us.

jonthehammer

I think that £18m is a lot of money to refuse for a club of our size. I will be really sad to see him go but if the club can pick up a top quality, solid centre-back for, say, £5m (i.e. Southgate), then we have money to strengthen other areas.

I would rather Rio had gone somewhere else, though, as I don't feel he will win much at Leeds and he deserves better.

daveoflondon

I'm sad he's going but £18m and the rumours of Gareth Southgate calm my nerves a bit. Good deal if money is spent wisely.

Alex G

At £18m it's a shame to lose Rio but with that money, and Harry's ability in the transfer market, I'm sure we're going to be all right . . .

But why the hell would Rio want to go to Leeds? It's not like they're a huge club, and their empire will come crashing down soon.

Gutted-hammer

Noooooooooooooooooooooooooooooooooooooooooooooo...

Carricks Pint

When the deal was going through I was a little annoyed that Rio had even spoken to Leeds.

Then, after seeing the player in tears leaving Chadwell Heath, my opinion changed 100 per cent.

I genuinely believe he did not want to go, but HR had a word in his ear and told him to take the opportunity. Of all the players that have since left WHU, I would sincerely applaud Rio's return, irrespective of the shirt he is wearing, simply because I believe he loves this club like the rest of us.

Grumpster

I think Rio is sheer class but even a non-selling club wouldn't be able to turn down that amount of money.

Only thing that annoys me is the fact that he's going to a club who I don't think are good enough for him and that probably hurts the most. But the boy has ambition, so I wish him well for the future.

simon.s

£18m? BITE THEIR BLOODY HAND OFF!

Lee S

£18m is a lot of money and West Ham could go and get

two decent players for that money.

However, I also compare it to the (Julian) Dicks sale when he went to Liverpool for £2m. I was young and remember ripping his picture off my wall, but it didn't really impact on us that much as a club. Perhaps this will be the same.

Talking to older members of my family, they just said that it had always been the West Ham way – Peters to Spurs in 1970 and Cottee to Everton in 1988 are just two examples.

Norn Iron Andy

Only one over-riding thought: WHY FECKING LEEDS?

Man U, I could understand. Arsenal or Liverpool, I could understand. Any of the top European teams, I could most definitely understand. But fecking Leeds? They ain't that much better than we are.

Rio, you could've gone anywhere you liked. Anywhere. Leaving West Ham for them bunch of white-shirted ****s is a real kick in the teeth. You can only have gone there for the money, because it certainly ain't to improve your footballing abilities or your trophy-winning chances.

BMU

'Brown views the youth academy as just another source of revenue'.

These prophetic words captured the feeling when, having told everyone that Rio was a cornerstone of the football club's development and progress, they accepted Leeds' bid of £18m.

I understand what people say when they look at £18m as a lot of money – but we believed we were developing something really special at West Ham, built around the greatest youth team ever assembled. The spine – from the defence to the creative midfield, with Kanouté and Di Canio up front with a young talent called Jermain Defoe coming on in leaps and bounds – gave genuine belief that, at last, we were going places.

When Brown sanctioned the sale of Ferdinand, we knew that this wasn't to be the last sale, that the West Ham board were driven by something other than making West Ham a great football team, and that this was yet another false dawn.

Rochford Hammer

I'm sad to see him go but it is a lot of money and, if spent wisely, it could be the making of the club.

West of London

I've lived in exile in Bradford for 11 years (job move, etc), so it was a sad day in old Westy's life to see Rio sign for Peter Ridsdale and his mega-underachievers. To see the heart of West Ham ripped out (or was it ripped off?), then paraded around Elland Road as a trophy, a symbol of how mighty Leeds are, and how crap and hard up West Ham are, is a bitter memory I will never forget.

Wiff

This transfer isn't just about the money. Every West Ham fan and player knows that as soon as Rio went for that amount, all the young players would be sold eventually, and that the chairman has no ambition but to sell the crown jewels. It's a signal to all clubs that West Ham is for sale . . .

Aiken Drum

I agree with others here. I don't want to see him go but for £18m, we'd be stupid to say no.

Everyone can see that the Sky bubble's going to burst soon and think of the kind of players we can get in with that sort of cash – even Brown can't pocket all of that without us noticing!

I know we'll get the old 'West Ham is just a selling club' lines thrown at us but every player has his price. Wenger has just sold Overmars, Petit is off and no one thinks Arsenal is on a downward spiral.

No, this will be good business and I wish the boy well for the future – just a shame it has to be Leeds really.

Alfs barnet

£18m? Who could turn that down? Good luck to him, he didn't want to go, but it's for the good of the club. Champions League within two years with that money.

Ged

£18 million is a phenomenal amount of money and if, as

suggested, the bottom is going to drop out of the transfer market, this is surely good business.

Sure, I don't want to see him go, but we could get a handful of decent players in for that money; perhaps a central defender who doesn't have the concentration span of a gnat?

cOOL cOL

This just goes to prove the ambition of our greedy board. I wonder how much Redknapp will get to spunk up the wall and how much of this will go in someone's pocket?

Tonka

With Christian Dailly and Rigobert Song forming an impressive partnership, Rio won't be missed.

By the way, the new stand is coming on great . . .

BLAGG, today

I was at the Docklands Arena watching the London Masters Football Tournament and ready to interview Frank McAvennie for West Ham Online when Rio Ferdinand was paraded before the Elland Road crowd. My mate Paul, Frankie M and myself watched the scenario unfold on the huge screens positioned under the Arena roof. How did I feel? About as low as I have ever felt since I started watching West Ham United – and believe me, that's pretty damn low!

Rio Ferdinand represented the new West Ham in the same way that Trevor Brooking, Bobby Moore and McAvennie himself had represented the old. My kids had signed photos of the man on their walls, Rio was a player who would pop up on MTV or BBC 'Yoof' programmes. My Mum knew who he was. Agreeing to sell Ferdinand to Leeds rather than waiting for the inevitable Man U, Barcelona or Real Madrid bid said more about the mentality of West Ham United Football Club than anything in the club's history.

It was a mistake of gargantuan proportions.

Rumours about the sale of Rio Ferdinand still do the circuit today. Despite my ranting at the time, there is now a school of thought that says that Harry Redknapp was principally behind the move and that Terence Brown was against it but followed the advice of his manager. That is why, so the theory goes, Brown later lost patience with Redknapp when his buys went seriously wrong. Unfortunately, neither ex-manager nor chairman has ever revealed the full reason for the sale.

Ferdinand represented Leeds for only a season-and-a-half before moving onto Manchester United for £30m – nearly twice the amount that West Ham received for him. During his stint at Leeds, Rio did play in the semi-final of the Champions League and many pundits believed that his general game improved, although Hammers fans are doubtful.

Rio moved to Old Trafford in July of 2002 as Leeds suffered from the fall-out of failing to qualify for the following season's premier European competition after their semi-final exit. In dire financial straits after the lavish spending of Peter Ridsdale and manager David O'Leary, they went to the brink of administration before being relegated from the Premiership in May 2004.

The transfer market is still in place, although the deal between Leeds and Man U represented the peak of the market. Had West Ham held on to Ferdinand for just two more seasons they could have doubled their money and possibly reaped some benefit on the field, as well as beyond it.

The subsequent collapse of Leeds United is matched only by that of West Ham.

Chapter 3

WHERE'S THE MONEY GONE?
May 2001

The sacking of Harry Redknapp in May 2001 was a major shock. That season's eventual 15th place finish (he went before the final game at Middlesbrough) was definitely a major disappointment in view of the squad of players that Redknapp had at his disposal but the general feeling was that West Ham and Harry Redknapp went together like Pie and Mash and this was just a blip on a generally upward trend.

However, at the time there were many who disagreed with my assessment that it was a mistake. Harry had seemingly lost all the money from Rio on some apparently bizarre transfers (and in truth the purchases of Rigobert Song and Titi Camara still look the acts of a desperate man even today) and there was a feeling that the club were underachieving with the players at our disposal.

Waters were muddied, though, by the fact that some of the sums didn't add up and there are suggestions that the Song and Camara deals had nothing to do with the Rio money which was, instead, ploughed into the new Dr Martens Stand. Many of us still refer to that side of the Boleyn Ground housing the museum and hotel as the Rio Ferdinand Stand.

Naturally, there were rumours of dark going-ons and wrong-doings by both manager and chairman but nothing has ever been proven. What really went on between them

31

that day in the boardroom may never be known.

Harry Redknapp's association with West Ham went back to the early 60s and the former winger was actually even more claret and blue than many younger fans realised. Redknapp was, by his own admission, 'a top-notch player at youth level'. In fact, Harry was part of the 1963 West Ham Youth Cup side that pulled back a 3-1 first leg deficit against Liverpool and, from being 2-1 down in the second leg, went on to lift the trophy. The gangling winger then went on to play for England's World Youth Cup side, helping win the trophy with a 4-0 trouncing of Spain in the final.

Redknapp's future looked secure when he joined his mate, Bobby Moore, in the Hammers first team and some people even predicted that Harry would join his World Cup-winning colleagues in the England set-up before long. But H never really developed as a player, showing maddening inconsistency in true Hammers style. One moment breathtaking, the next a ragged ginger pile in a heap, Redknapp became a cult celebrity on the terraces in that post-sarcastic way that only football fans can muster.

Songs were penned and sung with gusto by the North Bank choir and never more so than when Harry had an off night and performed on the pitch like a giraffe on ice. The newspapers, completely missing the fans' delicious ironic cheers as Redknapp crashed into the South Bank hoardings, took the songs and supporters' delight to be that of fans who had one of their own in their midst. Articles appeared proclaiming Redknapp to be a 'Hammers East End hero' and eventually fact blurred with fiction to provide a kind of 'king's new clothes' type of legacy. Ten years after he had retired, few could remember if Harry was any good or not.

But if there were doubts about Redknapp as a player, there were certainly no questioning his ability as a coach. His eye for a deal, his ability to handle players and his general bonhomie in dealing with the press, all made Harry good copy for the media. Consequently, his persona very much reflected West Ham's at the time and, although some were critical of his 'Jack the Lad' Cockney banter-style, others felt it bought some much-needed publicity to the club.

It's fair to say that even those who didn't support Redknapp were astonished at his dismissal.

The sacking of Redknapp also preceded the inevitable departure of his brother-in-law and No.2, Frank Lampard, which made his son, Frank Jnr's, position at the club virtually untenable. So another future England star was on his way out.

What made it even harder to bear was that it could have all been so different with a bit more luck and application.

The 2000-01 season had finished in disappointment after West Ham had memorably beaten Man U at Old Trafford and Premiership Sunderland at the Stadium Of Light to land a plum home draw against Spurs in the quarter-finals of the FA Cup. Many outsiders believed it was to be our year in the Cup. A home defeat in that game left a deep depression, though.

What made matters worse was that Redknapp publicly criticised the young Joe Cole for Spurs' second goal and many thought the criticism unwarranted and unfair. The league position had amounted to nothing but, in West Ham terms, there seemed no reason to view the 2000-01 campaign any differently to many others.

Terence Brown, though, obviously had other ideas.

BLAGG, May 2001

Last November West Ham sold their soul by accepting an £18m bid for Rio Ferdinand. On May 9, 2001, they decided to tear their heart out, too.

The 'mutual consent' sacking of Harry Redknapp is a sickening kick in the groin for our club and none of you should be in any doubt about it. I know there are a lot of people out there who thought that Harry had 'taken the club as far as he could', that his choice of assistant manager was nothing other than nepotism and that he seemed to think tactics were small white mints.

But, let's not fool ourselves too much. Because, while Harry may have had his shortcomings and some of the criticism may be justified, if nothing else, Harry Redknapp was one of us.

Harry lived and breathed claret and blue and always had the best interests of the club at heart. He may never be acknowledged as a great manager and, truth be told, he disappointed as a player, too, but he did his best for West

Ham United and I'm betting that today will be one of the saddest days in Harry's professional career.

The popular perception of Harry as a 'wheeler dealer' actually hid one of the great truths – the man was genuinely good at finding burgeoning talent and getting the best from players who had lost their way. Sadly, he was shafted by some ex-superstars who saw WHU as some sort of retirement home. But I reckon Harry's transfer record stands up to the best when you think what he had to work with. And that, for me, is the crux of the matter.

Harry, like many managers before him, was hamstrung by our board of directors. Do any of you really believe that H wanted to accept any amount of money for Ferdinand? Of course not! There are many, including myself, who would have preferred it if Harry had come right out and said as much but – well, it's not the West Ham way, is it?

Many of you will also argue that the Rio money has been wasted. Again, I wouldn't disagree – but let's not follow the party line from the *Evening Standard*. Harry hasn't wasted all the money from the transfer to Leeds. In fact, by my reckoning, there's still about £15m spirited away somewhere.

The truth is that if you sell one of the best central defenders in Europe, you can't take a one-eighth of the money received and replace him with a carbon copy. It doesn't work like that. Coventry City found that out to their cost last season. Like us, they couldn't turn down a ridiculous bid for striker Robbie Keane, so they accepted the money and now find themselves facing Crystal Palace and Watford in the First Division next season. Was it good business? Well, I'm no accountant but look at the amount received in TV fees alone for finishing 14th.

It genuinely amazes me how short-sighted these suited idiots in the directors' box can be. One of the criticisms thrown at these people is that they are not 'football folk', not 'workers' like you or me, but big businessmen who are only interested in balancing the books. So what businesses do they run then? What business allows you to sell your prize asset for £18m but then lose £25m because of the loss of that asset?

So why am I am lining up the board with regard to Harry?

Put simply, I do not believe that H departed the club by 'mutual consent'. I fear the only thing that would cause this is if Harry asked for some money, the board said 'No', and Harry said 'Well look, I can't work like this'.

I'm aware that there are worse rumours flying around claiming that Tricky Trev Sinclair and/or Frank Jnr are on their way out and Harry finally put his foot down over it. Quite frankly, I wouldn't discount any of them because, although many fans who visit WHO won't be sorry to see Harry go, his departure could be the very thin edge of an almost minuscule wedge.

I made my feelings known a few weeks back about any move to replace Redknapp. For me, there are no outstanding candidates and I'm really not heartened by the list of big names currently flying around. I can imagine Alan Curbishley will be everyone's favourite but will the return of Bluebottle ensure that someone like Frank Lampard or Paolo Di Canio be placated? Will AC on a tracksult draw the big stars of Europe? Will it 'eck as like! 'Bottle' may have done well at Charlton but yo-yoing between the top two divisions on a shoestring isn't what West Ham are looking for anymore. At least, I don't think it is – you'll have to check with Mr. Brown.

And let us not forget Curbishley buggered off to Birmingham City in his playing days, saying that 'West Ham lacked ambition'? Sound familiar? It would be the irony to end them all if Curbishley were offered the job but turned it down claiming Charlton are more progressive in their attitude.

I didn't think this season could get any worse and, foolishly, following our top-flight survival and the return of the classic 70s home shirt, I thought it might even improve.

But my hopes have been dashed today. I am really concerned for our immediate future and only hope this is down to my notorious pessimism. I've criticised Harry for his lack of media management – and I don't think he was above criticism in this and other areas – but I don't think he deserved what he got today. I genuinely feel for the man.

So, even if I am alone in this, I want to say a big THANK YOU to Harry Redknapp for turning this club around, nurturing a formidable youth set-up and giving me acres of quotes. Nobody can doubt that the man gave 100% and I thank him for that. If it's retirement (and I hope it is) for him, then I hope it's long and happy.

I'll always remember an 'Arry cross at speed by the corner flag and the resulting headed Pop Robson goal against Liverpool; a 9-0 (aggregate) FA Youth Cup win against Coventry; an Intertoto final win that brought European qualification; and a face that looked like a slab of condemned veal.

You were a fine West Ham man, Harry, and there's some who might criticise you for that – but I won't. Not here, not now.

Clarkie

I must admit I wanted Harry out. I was not his biggest fan but, even so, I was shocked to see him leave the way he did. The Board were ******* him with the Rio money and I think he left 'cos he wanted more cash to strengthen the team. As to who should be next manager, for me there is only one man and that is Alan Curbishley – just look at what he has done at Charlton with no money and players that are dog ****. Imagine what he could do with the players we've got. We could be challenging for Europe with Curbishley in charge.

Frankie

I was upset yesterday when the news filtered through. Harry has been in charge since I was 16 and I will miss the honesty of defeat and the smug smile when we win. Quite what the board are up to, I will never know but there's something not quite right about this. As for Curbishley – what are people on about? He's part of a yo-yo club who've fluked it all season. He's never had to handle any big names – except for Carl Leaburn, of course. I say go foreign, although that will cost a fortune and the club say they have no money.

Swiss Toni

Sentimental bollocks, Blagg. Pull yourself together man! Just get the right manager in and we'll be OK. It's a brave new world out there and we just need to get away from the

West Ham management tradition and try for something different. We will sink or swim. No time for lifebuoys.

HR From Down Under

We were in a real bind with Harry. We know his post-match slagging off of our players and his tactical ineptness made him seem unfit to be a manager but, for some reason or other, the majority of our players seemed to love him. I would have kicked him upstairs as Head of Recruitment and got in a real coach rather than an Arfur Daley wheeler-dealer used car salesman. Mind you, he would probably have quit anyway.

NorthBanker

Why does Blagg refer to Curbishley as Bluebottle?

Neilson

You must be a young 'un here, NorthBanker. Blagg is referring to the staggering likeness between our ex-midfield maestro and possible next manager and the puppet used in TV's *Telegoons* back in the 60s. See here for an explanation: http://www.bbc.co.uk/comedy/guide/articles/t/gallery/telego onsthe_7774305_1.shtml

Nimods

Isn't this just pure West Ham, though? You look at Paolo Di Canio and you think H was a genius in the market place. Then you look at Gary Charles and you wonder what the hell he must be thinking of. When Davor Suker played for Arsenal, H drooled over how lucky the Arse were to be able to have a player like that in their squad "He'd walk into anyone's first team". We all nodded agreement. A year later he's a West Ham player and we never see him. He's over the hill. We all go "yeah, he is". This goes on so often it's like watching a magic show – we don't know what's real and what's not. I think it was time for a change, so I'm not too upset to see 'Arry go but I'm just worried if this isn't just another illusion and we'll look back at this in a few years time and wonder why the club sacked him.

Tim Johnson
West Ham should rename themselves Wet Sham after the shabby way they ended the season. Harry was not the reason they failed.

Bill from Barnet
Billy, you are talking crap.

Goody-Ireland
I agree with Billy, well said, mate. I am also really concerned about what happens next. I mean, there is not much choice of good managers out there at the moment. I am not convinced by Curbishley, Graham, etc. Are there any other candidates?

Also I wish Harry all the best – he was a great servant to the club.

North of Watford
Spare a thought for the West Ham players right now. Professional footballers they may be, but when the choirmaster gets shown the door of the vestry, how do you persuade the choiristers to go on singing? And from the same hymn book? The next manager has a fair bit of conducting to do, trying to coax his talented individuals to sing in tune. There'll be a fair bit of arm-waving in rehearsals, but let's hope they sing like birds by the time of their next performance. After all, they do take home around 20 grand a week on average – a bit better than your average choirboy.

Dirty from Chafford 100
I feel for Harry.

If there was a better man out there to come and take over it may have been justified but, as we will find out the hard way, there isn't, not for a club like West Ham that has to improve the squad on a shoestring.

Thank you, Harry, for providing some football over the last few years that we will never forget.

Daren
How can you say the problems with the end of season

scare were Harry's fault. Rio was sold – and it wasn't Harry's choice, he wouldn't have sold Rio.

Maybe if Rio was still in the team we wouldn't have had the bad results at the end of the season. We may have also done Spurs and got to the Cup final.

Who can say?

Iain Dowie's Love Child

SImple logIc here, nobody resigns from their job just one game before the end of a season and the following holiday. He was shot as sure as JR was.

Martin

I bet all the people hoping for Curbishley as the new manager were the same people who booed him for two years when he passed the ball sideways to another West Ham player 20 years ago.

Lady Hammer

God bless Harry, and Frank too. You have given us years of pleasure, and we love you for it.

I only hope that all of the morons who wanted you out realise what they have lost and what a can of worms has now been opened by your departures.

GOD HELP US ALL. I cannot see any of the youngsters staying now that their 'Second Dad' has gone, they must all feel as bad as FLJ. I cannot bring myself to renew my season ticket until I know exactly what is going on. Does anyone else feel the same way? I feel worse than when Rio left and I STILL feel gutted about that.

Oh please, someone help take away the sadness that I am feeling now! PLEASE!!!!

Down to bare bones

The board had no other choice but to get rid of Redknapp. His good seasons counted for nothing when he has nearly got the club relegated. The board could see that he could take the club no further and could not take the risk of relegation next season. They had to look at this from a business viewpoint and not let sentiment get in the way. They had no choice.

Gutted-hammer

Harry gone?
Noooooooooooooooooooooooooooooooooooooooooooooooo...

East side Eric

'Down to bare bones' – dead right, mate. Relegation would
have been devastating. I think some fans don't actually
appreciate what would happen:

1) The loss to the club would be £15-20m per year.

2) We could not afford the wages and our best players
would be sold to pay for the ground improvements, which
have gone too far to be cancelled.

3) We could not have attracted the quality players needed
to get back into the Premiership.

We are talking big bucks in football nowadays. There's no
room for sentiment. Sad, but that's life.

Rainham Pete

He may have had his faults but he only strived to assemble
our best squad ever. His reaction to the sale of (Andy) Impey
and Rio echo that.

Yes, this season was a painful one to watch, full of promise
and then bugger all, as usual. Was HR solely to blame? –
who knows, How much of a contributing factor did the
injuries play? . . . the Rio sale? . . . the poor buys?
Collectively they all played a part.

All his critics got their wish. The Redknapp era is at an end
– and now the future. We have a bigger stadium and a shite
new kit but what manager worth his salt will go to a club
that lacks vision, with little or no £££s to spend? How can
we expect to retain the likes of Cole, Carrick and Defoe who
burn with ambition?

In my opinion, the future of the club all hangs on the
appointment of Mr X. Will it be a high profile manager with
£12m to spend, new tactics and success . . . or are we set
to become another Wimbledon?

MikeyD

Very sad/angry to see Harry pushed out. OK, this season's
been bad but we had three top 10 places and a European
run before that, so I can forgive Harry one bad year.

We've missed (Steve) Lomas and (Trevor) Sinclair badly and need a 20-goal-a-year man as well as a better defence. I was already looking forward to next year and would not swap our stars (anyone who thinks Lampard should go is a twat. We need goals from midfield – and Frank gets 'em) for anyone. We're very close to being a bloody good team.

Look at the goal difference – top 6 = +20, bottom 4 = -20 and everyone else very close. We're better than a lot of teams who finished above us (Charlton were outplayed twice).

Bottom line is, Harry should have stayed and we gotta hang on to what we got.

Petert

Cast your mind back to when H took over. We were crap and sinking fast. Harry bought some really dodgy players in his time and, to be honest, his tactics weren't the best in the league. But he will go down for me as the man who saved West Ham and reinvented everything the claret and blue stands for; inconsistent, maddening but, at times, able to take your breath away by reaching levels of skill to take on the very best. Thanks H and good luck, mate.

Upton Spark

Blagg, you are not alone in wanting to thank a man who has done so much for the club. However, I hope he stays in the game at a decent level – he is a good manager and if he wants a job I hope he gets one.

Hammer Boy

Harry gone, nice bloke but he has wasted the Rio money. He agreed to Rio's sale and has not stopped whingeing since. Sorry Blagg, you are wrong. This is a sad day but the future is better. I cannot believe that the board had the guts to sack Harry – they have gone up in my estimation. My only regret is he has spent so much of the Rio money on crap.

Mr Egg

Harry wasted the Rio money, eh?
£2m Song, £1.5m Camara, £0.5m Todorov, £2.5m Dailly. Not many of you got a calculator?

Saitchy

I heard someone on the radio last night saying he was turning cartwheels of joy at Harry's departure and it showed the board were, at last, showing signs of being fed up with our lack of success. I think it shows more that the board want success on a shoestring.

Success is a relative thing. As someone who has year after year started every season wondering if we were going to be relegated, the last three seasons have been a great success in my eyes. What we now need to do is build on it.

This season has been a blip and Harry rightly sees that we need to bolster the squad. We were hit by long-term injuries that damaged our performances. Looking at Harry's transfer dealing shows an overall net profit of £11m. If you remove the Rio cash from the equation, it means break even, because £7m was spent after Rio was sold. How many other clubs have done as much with a net break even in the transfer market?

Much has been made of the poor buys since Rio was sold. Christian Dailly, Rigobert Song and Titi Camara haven't set the world on fire but how much is down to the fact that Harry needed three players and was limited in how much he could spend, so took a gamble?

The biggest mistake he made was letting Hannu Tihinen slip through his fingers, saying he was overpriced at £4m. If Rio was worth £18m, how could Hannu not have been worth £4m? He should have bought Hannu instead of Dailly and Song – better to have one consistently good player than two who are inconsistent and mediocre.

Perhaps it is the case that Harry has taken us as far as he can, but I will not listen to any denigration of his impact on the success of the club.

I wouldn't cry my eyes out to see Frank Jnr go. If we get £12m for him, we should surely be able to get a great left-sided midfielder and look at a midfield of Sinclair, Carrick, Cole and AN Other. I wouldn't weep if Kanouté went either. He's been okay but hasn't been the 20-goals-a-season man we need. Let's see if Jermain Defoe can move up and score 20.

Let's look forward and give the new manager our support – I hope it is Curbs.

Ol BLue Eyes

Billy, you've lost the plot, you're still wearing those rose
tinted glasses reading Mills and Boon, aren't you?

Harry could cope three-to-five years ago but the game has
moved on and he hasn't shown any ability to change with
the times. Yes, gratitude for what he has achieved, but also
this year he has been crap. We can't hide from that – he
takes the credit where it's due but also the brickbats.

Gerry

I am feeling totally betrayed by the board, and not for the
first time either.

AdamL

Hear, hear, Billy. Redknapp did a great job whilst he was
here. The board didn't. If Harry asked for £15m to spend
over the summer, and the board said no, then that is a
disgrace. We still have that left from the Rio sale.

Wattie

It's a tough old world, Billy. In football, like in other areas of
sport, business, politics, etc. you are judged by your results.
From the heady days of 1999, when the team finished fifth in
the Premiership (but still had dubious form along the way) to
now, there has been an increase in talent, but a marked
decline in form. It is as if the players no longer believe in the
cause, they lack not ability but motivation. The fact remains
that provided the players have ability, the manager has the
ultimate responsibility for performance.

Harry has done wonders for West Ham, I've said this here
previously. He's turned the club from First Division obscurity
into a Premiership force. He's put millions into the coffers
and developed a fine crop of youngsters for the future, plus
he's breathed new life into wrecks on the soccer scrapheap.
He has also made very big and expensive mistakes in the
transfer market.

Even so, I wish Harry was still at West Ham, but in the role
of general manager (like David Pleat at Spurs). The West
Ham board has a lot to answer for. There may be worse to
come – I expect FLJ and Kanouté are packing up their
sports kits right now. It's a tough old world!

Nash

H did do a great job with the youth and some transfers but he was a victim of his own success. He was good when he had a good player in each position but when he had a squad to pick from, he panicked and did nothing tactically.

I don't care if FLJ goes 'cos I think he was on his way soon anyway. For every Kanouté/Di Canio/Sinclair/Hartson H has bought, he also bought a Camara/Raducioiu/Dumitrescu/Charles/Suker, etc. And while the good ones he got were well supplemented by the youth players, you can't keep buying the likes of Camara and expect the fans and board to be impressed.

I think the board held back money 'cos his record wasn't as good as some people made out and his insistence that 'Psycho' (Stuart Pearce) could do no wrong got a bit boring and inaccurate.

Ta, H, and thanks for the set-up – but no regrets in you leaving.

W.E

Let's not get too sentimental about Harry going, eh? Yes, he's worked wonders turning us into a top Premier side. And yes, he gave us PDC. But this season he really lost the plot. His tactics were crap, his signings were worse and he only used subs to keep the bench warm. It's time we started to go forward and actually try to win some silverware. So come on board, appoint the right man and give him the funds to get West Ham into the big time.

Saphron

I don't want his replacement to have 'Claret and Blue' in his veins, as I don't want this to happen again in a few years time. I want an efficient manager who couldn't give a toss about anything but getting results and living or dying by them. The team and the youth set-up has the talent to deliver and play 'attractive' football, so now I want the results and I want the next manager to be a right bastard and get them.

I always liked Harry, still do, always will. But compare him to Ferguson or O'Leary, you don't think Man U or Leeds fans would actually LIKE their manager if they weren't producing the goods, do you?

For that reason, I can't bear the thought of another of West Ham's favourite sons being at the helm, someone who I'd gladly invite into my house. Instead, I want a coldly ruthless and efficient bastard who, if he doesn't get the results, can fully expect to be shown the door and receive the riot act from the fans.

Ginger Iron

Harry should definitely go down as one of the greats at West Ham. I am gutted he has gone, although he made mistakes this season.

Lady J

Well said, Blagg. Old, condemned veal features may not have been a great manager, but it's going to be hard to replace him with someone as loyal to the club as he was.

Dave

Maybe Harry deserved a place within the club somewhere but let's face it, he had **** all to do with the coaching of the youth teams and can't claim all the credit for the quality of our kids.

He bought too many bad buys, fell out with too many good players and just lost the plot. We are stronger without him and a new broom will move us forward, not backwards, where Harry was taking us.

Don't lose sight of the fact that our top 10 finishes have been with very low point totals and, give or take a couple of wins, we would have been bottom 10 for the last four seasons. And no Cup wins either. Thanks for what you did, H, but that's where it ends.

Paul d

West Ham will qualify for the Champions League if we get Alan Curbishley as manager

Oscar

Good, good piece Blagg, says a lot that some dicks have missed while they gloated over H leaving. Seeing the photos of him leaving was quite upsetting and I realised I, and I think the club, are going to miss him. More depressingly judging from the papers, and not just the scummy red tops, it looks like all our worst fears may be realised. Curbishley is OK but hardly earth-shattering. Next season could be a long struggle.

armchair
Good article. I'm in total agreement – very shoddy business. Good luck, Harry!

Knobby
Don't let the fact that there are 'no obvious better candidates' out there cloud your judgement. Harry was out of his depth and managed to turn the much-quoted best squad in 20 years into relegation material.

Fresh blood, fresh ideas, man-management skills and an understanding of tactics are what we need, and Curbs and any one of a number of available people offer that. Our problem has always been that we have accepted failure and anyone still backing Redknapp are proof of that.

Walky
Harry is a top bloke and did turn the club around over the last seven years. Maybe he couldn't take the club any further but he deserves credit for what he did. Good luck, Harry. I also feel pessimistic for the short-term future of the club

GMAN
Yeah, he may be one of us, but he was no good at the job. Just because he's a WHU man through and through doesn't qualify you to be the manager.

BLAGG, today
My fears were uncannily accurate and for several months I went around suspecting that I may be distantly related to Mystic Meg (same hairstyle and faraway glazed look).

Alan Curbishley was approached but opted to stay at Charlton for reasons too frightening to contemplate. Similarly, Steve McClaren was sounded out but, again, West Ham got a refusal and he left his position as Alex Ferguson's assistant at Man U to become manager of Middlesbrough instead.

Then came a worrying silence that seemed to drift on for months, fertile ground for rumour and counter-rumour.

Within a few weeks, West Ham had been linked to virtually every coach ever to plug in a PlayStation, load up Championship Manager and take Crewe Alexandra to the Champions League final. World Cup-winning names were touted and foreign coaches whom no one had ever heard of were suddenly becoming household names around Upton Park.

The fans were starting to get worried. The feeling was that Redknapp had been sacked on the assumption that Curbishley would take the role. But now that Plan A had failed to materialise, was there a Plan B?

The answer was worse than we dared hope. There was not a Plan B but there was a Plan Z version 3.2 . . .

Chapter 4

LOS GLENNDOS
June 2001

Glenn Roeder was confirmed as Harry Redknapp's successor at West Ham United on June 14, 2001, having been appointed as caretaker boss following Redknapp's shock departure in May.

Roeder was actually brought into the club as a coach by Redknapp in 1999, having previously worked in Glenn Hoddle's England set-up. Highly rated by Hoddle during his time as the national coach, Roeder was regarded as an up and coming coach with substantial league experience from a career that spanned 574 games and earned him seven caps as an England 'B' international.

Although Glenn Roeder was a Hammers fan as a boy, he began his playing career with near neighbours Leyton Orient before joining Queens Park Rangers, where he appeared 157 times, going on to captain the side under boss Terry Venables and appearing in an FA Cup final against Spurs. He later moved to Newcastle United in 1984, where he became a mentor to the young Paul Gascoigne. Roeder enjoyed a successful five-year spell at St James' Park before joining Watford and then Gillingham at the end of his playing career.

*Appointed Gills' manager for one season before being
invited to take over as Watford manager following Steve
Perryman's exit from Vicarage Road, Roeder was in charge
of the Hornets for nearly three years. He took the team to
within one place of the play-offs in 1994-95.*

*But the following season was not so successful and
Roeder left the club in February 1996 with Watford in dire
trouble. They were relegated at the end of that season.*

*However, Roeder's coaching talents were appreciated at
Upton Park where he helped nurture some of the most
promising youth players such as Joe Cole and Michael
Carrick. Rumours persisted at the time that the younger
players asked the board to consider Roeder for the job while
some of the senior players were apparently unconvinced.*

*Whatever the politics, there is little doubt that many fans
had hoped for the appointment of a bigger name.*

*The day and time I discovered that Glenn Roeder had been
appointed manager of West Ham United is something I
doubt I will ever forget.*

BLAGG, June 2001

This is a Billy Blagg Public Service announcement to all
West Ham Online readers yet to go on holiday this year. I
feel it only fair to inform you of a new greeting sweeping
mainland Europe – and probably, by the time you read this,
the Americas too. Lacking a name for this new
acknowledgement, I have decided to call it 'Los Glenndos'.

The greeting starts with the normal cry to attract the
attention: 'Oy Mate', 'ere Geeezza' or, possibly, 'Hey
Cockernee Bastardo'. Once your attention has been gained
the assailant will then shout at the top of his voice: 'Glenn
Roeder!' this is then followed either by a signal resembling
the world-famous thumbs-down gesture or, on occasion, a
final flourish involving peals of laughter.

As I decided to sport the rather natty new Fila kit on the
Costa Dorado last week, I was subject to this new greeting
on several occasions and I can assure you I never tired of
the warm feeling of belonging that it invoked. You're going to
enjoy this one on holiday all summer, so do try and wave
and grin back, won't you?

In my scrapbook of West Ham memories, I don't think I will

ever forget the morning that I discovered the identity of our new supremo. Following a heavy session at an all-night salsa bar, Lady Blagg and I decided to round the evening off nicely with a huge barney involving lots of bad language, tantrums and childish posturing (the good lady is not a person improved by the consumption of a few cold beers). We stormed off to bed, subsequently overslept and found ourselves in a post-breakfast situation the following morning.

Now the good woman and I are normally fairly cultured travellers and we tend to shy away from places such as Salou's Big Ben Breakfast Bar. However, to coin a cliché, beggars can't chose their breakfasts, so it was a swift stagger over the road for a 'Full Monty and don't spare the fried bread'.

Ploughing through the assorted English papers that came with breakfast, I noted Arsenal's purchase of one of my pre-Harry recommendations, Francis Jeffers; quickly spotted that Frank Jnr had gone to Chelsea for £11m and was quietly perusing a picture of our lad in a Chelsea strip when the face on the opposite page caught my eye.

Was that Glenn Roeder in a suit and a hard hat?

And was that pile of rubble an indication of West Ham's aspirations this season?

Surely they haven't, have they? They can't have! But they had . . .

Lady Blagg will confirm my initial response was: "That's relegation sitting there", before flinging the paper across the table, narrowly missing Lady B's 'Tea like Muvva makes' and restarting the previous evening's row again. However, if nothing else, the good lady knows that, where me and West Ham are concerned, there's no arguing and she wisely elected to leave me to stew for the rest of the morning.

I found a few Spanish cats and proceeded to kick them around.

I ached to get onto the Internet, call up Online and see what the immediate responses were from you lot. I must have written a dozen columns in my head as well – and none of them were without bad language. However, a few hours in the sun and a couple of cool *cervezas* later, I managed to calm down and view things rationally.

The fact is that the appointment of Glenn Roeder is disappointing. Obviously, the man wasn't the first choice, otherwise he would have been appointed the day after Harry left. It seems incredible that we couldn't attract a bigger name but, when push comes to shove, should we be surprised?

I think I've almost fallen victim to my own press and believed that this time West Ham were really going to get a grip and push us in the 21st century. But the fact is that Glenn is no bigger name than Harry was when he took over, no more a certainty to succeed than Billy Bonds, more likely to be accepted than Macari and, possibly, may be the best real coach we've had at the club since John Lyall. In short, this may lead us into the fairyland of relegation but maybe – just maybe – we might get a break for once.

I was initially annoyed that I was away during the one week that West Ham appoints a new manager but reading through Online on my return, I wonder if it might not be a blessing in disguise. It's given me time to sit back and think about the real situation rather than the one in my head. If I'd been here I would have blasted off an offensive piece, blaming the board as usual, but now I can take some time out to reflect on the bigger picture (I sound like a Middle Manager in the City).

I won't pretend I wasn't excited by a the mooted arrival of a French World Cup-winning manager or a Euro-winning Italian boss but, in truth, outside of the 'big boys', who can lay claim to one of these men? The rest of the Premiership stumbles on with a Reid or a Burley so why should we think we are being hard done by? Glenn Roeder has a lot to prove and his desire to succeed may even work in our favour. He's young. He's keen. Apparently, Glenda Doddle appreciated his coaching acumen. Hey! I'm starting to even get enthusiastic about it, aren't you? No, I thought not . . .

At the moment it seems that Glenn Roeder has been handed a poisoned chalice but I think it would be nothing less than plain mean spirited not to wish the man all the luck in the world. It's so tempting to add the caveat 'you're gonna need it' but I'm not going to go down that route.

I don't think I'm going to get a real feeling for what we can expect until a few transfer deals have been tied up. I know

the cry is up already that Glenn is nothing more than a
puppet of the board – and I can certainly see that argument
being difficult to refute. But the fact is that the man has been
appointed and given the FLJ £11m plus £4m from the Rio
transfer (whaddya mean, what happened to the other £14m
– haven't you seen Titi Camara, Rigobert Song, Christian
Dailly and that nice new Castle turret on the Boleyn
forecourt?).

He seems to have some ideas. He seems to have the
respect of most of the squad and I've even heard that he's a
disciplinarian with a dim view of poor training methods. So,
who knows? Perhaps we have taken a step forward.

Whether it's a step over a precipice, only time will tell.

BLAGG, today

*It was interesting to gauge the fans' comments just a week
after Roeder's appointment. The shock and disappointment
that followed the immediate announcement had been
replaced with a typical Cockney stoicism or, at the very least,
a resigned shrug.*

*Within a short time the inevitable transfer rumours began.
German European champion Olivier Beirhoff was strongly
linked with the club as was, more surprisingly, the England
No.2 goalkeeper, David James. Sebastian Schemmel, a
player Harry Redknapp had tried and rejected, was acquired
on a free transfer, suggesting that Roeder was his own man.
Things were moving.*

*The inevitable breath of fresh air that always accompanies
a change at the top was beginning to make itself felt and it
seemed to be reflected in supporters' attitudes.*

Goodster

Roeder sounds like he knows what he wants and who he
wants and won't give up until he has them. Who thought
when he was appointed that he would sign a current
England international? Because I know I didn't.

After the initial shock, I'm really beginning to change my
mind about Roeder. I really thought the board had made a
MASSIVE mistake with him. But so far, so good. I know the
season hasn't started yet and things could go pear shaped,
but as we speak things are looking 100 per cent better than

they did a few weeks ago. I really think that many of us are now ready to give him a chance. Who really believed they would be thinking that?

I know the board was really impressed with what Roeder had to say when they interviewed him and the many ideas he had. Well, he doesn't look to be too bad and maybe, just maybe, the board do know what they are doing.

I know it could all go tits-up come the end of September, but we MUST give him and the team a chance and see what happens.

Mad Dog

Well, I'm still not convinced – the proof will be how the team plays. However, I haven't slated him yet. Just worried about his CV.

Macca

He will be judged on results but he's more my idea of a modern football coach than Redknapp will ever be. The days of the Ron Atkinson/Barry Fry/Dave Bassett wheeler-dealer are long gone, and Harry has gone with them I think.

Roeder has shown a lot of common sense and, to be fair, realism. He knows we're not a top six side but there is a lot of potential there which needs to be built on. He looks like he's toughening up training. He must have got some tactical awareness from working with Hoddle at England. He's bought two decent players (including a current England international) for less money than Redknapp blew on Song and Camara. He hasn't put a foot wrong yet. Even the sale of Lampard, for what you have to say is an extraordinary amount of money, doesn't seem to be a disaster at present.

Fair play to him and good luck, I say.

Woody

So West Ham are in trouble! Well, that's what everyone keeps saying, but I don't see it that way. We have just had a wake up call and a swift kick, now we have the chance to correct the problems in the team.

Harry Redknapp may have gone but maybe that is a good thing for the club. He has taken us as far as he can and last season proved his time was up.

The appointment of Glenn Roeder may upset a few people who expected a big name manager, but they forget that big names were once rookies in terms of football and everybody has to make their start somewhere.

I think that Roeder will pull off a cracker and finish in the top 10 next season and, to be honest, I am more worried about the board than I am the manager, because in the end you are only as good as the players you manage. Having some players does help, not selling them all the time.

OK, so Rio, Lamps and big, bad Psycho have gone and now we feel wounded. So what, let's get over it and carry on and keep producing more talented youngsters. Rio and Lamps chose lesser teams to play for – give it two or three years and we will be a top five team and they would have missed out.

GeoffT

Roeder's making the right noises and I've a feeling he'll only bring in players, like James, who are better than what we have already – unlike Harry, who brought in players just to enlarge the squad.

Fizz

James would not have come to us if he was not assured we are not going to sell any more of the young talent at West Ham. He left Villa because he criticised the manager and Doug Ellis. GR is not bringing in dead wood or taking gambles. Redknapp loved a bet and he did it with some of his buys. Yes, he had one or two winners but like all gamblers, he lost more than he won. Roeder is making a very good start, so let him take his time and get it right. He is building a defence to stop the silly goals we conceded last season by starting with a goalkeeper who plays for England and a good French defender. Positive stuff.

Steve

I'm the first to admit that I'm not, and never will be, convinced that Roeder should have ever been appointed West Ham manager but that's not the reason for my absence from Upton Park this season.

That reason is a group of accountants, bank managers and

solicitors who have had a stranglehold on the club for too long.

Ironman

OK, Glenn has made a semi-good signing by getting James but the bloke's been in charge six weeks now and this is all we've got to show for it. Personally, I feel there was no need for another keeper with Shaka, Forrest and Bywater already here.

I agree with most of you that Rodeo has been like a breath of fresh air recently but I tend to think were getting a little carried away. All that's really changed is Glenn gave a good interview which, we all agreed, answered some of our frustrations, and we've signed a keeper.

Cardiff Irons

I think any criticism of Roeder is a reflection on the fact that we've had a pretty torrid time of it in the last few months.

If we're going to get on Roeder's back the minute we go 1-0 down in our first home game, then we might as well pack him in now. Imagine going into a new job yourself and then, when you make your first cock-up, the boss sitting behind you says: "I knew he was no good, said he'd blow it".

I think the initial uproar about Roeder was much more to do with the way the board went about things, than a reflection on Roeder. Most people on this site have prefaced their (justified) ranting about the way the club is being run with the words "nothing against GR, but . . ."

At the end of the day, the board wildly raised expectations that we were now a big-time club and that we would be getting a big-name manager. I think that was a charade and I also think the appointment of GR was in their minds long before they announced it. A classic case of raising expectations amongst the fans and then dashing them. If the board expected that to go down quietly, then they're clearly more inept than even I thought they were.

GR has (and will) receive some of the backlash because he is the most visible part of the West Ham set-up but GR and the team have my support.

The Virus

He's shown that he deserves the chance so far. I mean, players training a full day? After training, he's staying back to work on more plans? Unheard of for some years now, but bloody welcome. He's brought a good off the field attitude and more professional approach so far. So with the season yet to start (and so no results to judge him by, which is what really counts), he must be given the thumbs up.

Lukie

I've not changed my mind about Roeder, I'm just a little more optimistic. I don't feel he's done anything a proven big name manager couldn't have also done, if not better. I am happy with the signing of James and will be even happier if we land Bierhoff, as rumours suggest.

Having heard the quotes from Roeder, it is very apparent that he's on a hiding to nothing. He knows that, and he knows if results don't go his way, he'll be out. I like the way he's approached the whole situation and his general way of conducting business, compared to HR's, is excellent. I'm going to wait 'till these two new signings are with us before I make a prediction and statement on the new season and Roeder as our manager. For the moment, I've been appeased. Things could be a lot worse but they could also be better. Let's just wait and see!

Nels

It's not that I'm convinced the board have made the right appointment, 'cos I'm not. It's just that we're all West Ham and we tend to gather round and pull the wagons together when any of us are attacked. My attitude is, the appointment has been made and there's nothing we can do about it so let's just get on with it, get behind Roeder – who is at least 'one of us' – and hope it all comes right.

Like Blagg, I don't really see the difference between this appointment and that of Johnny Lyall. And he did all right, didn't he?

Miss G

I agree with Nels. I was hoping for a bigger name and can't make out if the promises for a big-time boss were in our head or if the board had really thought they could get someone else. But Glenn's in charge now and I'll give him 100 per cent support and keep my fingers crossed.

Gutted Hammer
Roeder? Noooooooooooooooooooooooooooooooo...

Chapter 5

THE ROCKY ROED AHEAD
Season 2001-02

Nothing is more likely to show the pernicious nature of the average football fan than to chart the lives of those following the fortunes of West Ham United for all bar a handful of seasons over the past 40 years.

By definition, this is all about Glenn Roeder's first season in charge of West Ham but, in another way, it is the story of the club under differing regimes and in different decades. Good results, bad results, players look good, players look bad, manager looks competent and in control, manager looks like he has only ever managed a Subbuteo side before.

Supporter argued against supporter as, under Roeder, the claret and blue managed to turn inconsistency into an art form. Arguments among fans during this period were brisk and uncompromising, falling into two quite distinctive camps. The first group believing Roeder should be given a chance and that things looked as if they were on the up, while the other believed, sooner or later, that it would all end in tears.

In hindsight, it all looks fairly cut and dried but such was the astonishing ability of the team to combine inept performances one week with solid displays the next that nobody was entirely sure if this was a team finding its feet under a new director or a mob adrift with little clue and no guidance. We may never know.

The 2001-02 season began with an almost inevitable opening 2-1 defeat at Anfield. This was followed by some fairly uninspiring draws, a home win and more away defeats. It wasn't immediately apparent but a tone was being set for the season, although it didn't help that summer signing, David James, broke his leg playing for England before he had even kicked a ball for the Hammers.

Under Roeder, West Ham began to look impregnable at home - 'Fortress Upton Park' became a watchword - while the epithet 'shambles' could equally be applied to the same team on its travels. As a supporter it was difficult to fathom why the same team could be responsible for such differing results every week.

The more tactically astute among the fans reckoned that the West Ham way was only able to work at home where the structure of the side enabled them to put visitors under increasing pressure. Away from home, though, the same pattern meant players, particularly Paolo Di Canio, drifted through games with seemingly little direction or hope. Away form reached a nadir with two appalling results in late September and early October 2001, at Blackburn and Everton, that seemed to spell relegation well before James took his place at the expense of Shaka Hislop.

BLAGG, October 2001

The last thing you need when you are dog-tired and in desperate need of sleep is to find yourself at a computer keyboard in the early hours of the morning trying to make sense of a 7-1 pasting. Is 'pasting' even the right word? If a 5-0 defeat is a 'rout' or an 'embarrassment', then what is a seven-goal hiding? Feel free to write and tell me – I'd really like to know.

Still, if nothing else, I am a martyr to the cause so here I am again with witty and incisive insights into what is really happening at West Ham. And what exactly is occurring?

Well, the new Doc Martens stand is coming on well and soon we shall have one of the best castle turrets to be seen outside of the National Trust. Soon after work will begin on the other side of the ground and Terence Brown will be able to boast to the chairmen of visiting sides about the incredible financial wizardry that enabled a poor East End side to own such a magnificent edifice. It's debatable if the chairman of Chesterfield or Grimsby will be quite as impressed as Lord Terry himself but thems the breaks, eh?

So the question we have to ask ourselves now is: are there three clubs worse than us in the Premiership at the moment? And then, when we've finished laughing, we have to ask how we are going to go about ensuring that we drag ourselves above at least three come next spring. Because that's what we are talking about here. Forget Cup runs and late European surges. If we get through this season with our Premiership status still intact, then we will have done well.

So how bad are our players? Well, for me, the answer has to be 'not that bad at all really'. We've got problem areas, sure, but there must be more than the lack of a dominant defender to explain a staggering 12 goals conceded in two matches.

So what about the team spirit? Well, Trevor Sinclair answered that for me last week by his sickening request for a transfer. Why would a player who had just broken into the England squad ask for a transfer to increase his England chances? The answer is, of course, it has nothing to do with filling in the difficult left midfield role for England but more to do with playing in a crumbling excuse of a Premier team. Even Glenn Roeder had to admit that "Trevor had been unsettled ever since Rio Ferdinand left", so it seems that only Tricky Trev's injury last year prevented this becoming public knowledge earlier.

How I dearly wish that I could write a Blagg column without mentioning those two words 'Rio' and 'Ferdinand'. The whole club has become cursed since the arrival of £18m big ones and the irony is further cemented by Rio's diabolical performance against Greece where he looked every inch the – supposedly – under-performing Hammers centre-half of old. So much for the low-lights of darkest Yorkshire.

Still, Rio's gone. So has the money from his sale and that of Frank Jnr. So where do we go from here? Well, I really hate to say this because I really feel for the bloke, but you have to wonder how much longer we can carry on with Glenn Roeder at the helm. No one has backed the man more than me but these defeats are a bit more than just run-of-the-mill knock backs. These are humiliating maulings at the hands of teams who we are going to be our main rivals for relegation next May.

When Glenn was appointed I mentioned him being passed a poisoned chalice but, after Everton and Blackburn, GR must feel as if the man who handed him the chalice has now set about him with the silver tray as well. I'm not one to call for managerial changes – and probably couldn't suggest a decent replacement anyway – but we can't go on like this.

A look at the fixture list shows a 'must win' game against Southampton on Saturday followed by a month in which we have Chelsea, Fulham and Tottenham as visitors while we make the short trip to Charlton and the 'not really up north' trek to Ipswich. These are games that the players at this club should be capable of winning if their mindset is right and, rightly or wrongly, that is where we now have to look.

I'm sorry, Glenn, but the fickle finger of fate points at you.

Make no mistake about it, this is one vital month.

BLAGG, today

Just 10 days later everything was rosy again. Proof that supporting West Ham can make an idiot of anyone (particularly someone brave, or silly, enough to try writing about them every week).

BLAGG, Nov 2001

Two wins – one not entirely convincing and the other a rip-roaring, nailbiting, knees-up   have made the Boleyn a much happier place this week. It would be a hard man who didn't feel some vindication for Glenn Roeder. It's not unreasonable to ask serious questions about a side that has lost games by 5-0 and 7-1 – indeed, I asked a few myself – but you can do no more than answer with some victories.

There's been a lot of petty sniping, bad mouthing and disinformation coming from ex-players, ex-managers and any journalist within reach of a keyboard this last month but it's amazing how this stops immediately the team starts winning. Call me stupid, but I fancy an away win coming up. When it does I will say 'well done Glenn' and be quite happy to eat any humble pie that Mr. Roeder fancies sending me. I hope others are man enough to do likewise.

BLAGG, today

*And an away win did, indeed, arise with a good victory at
(then) European-bound Ipswich. A home game against
Fulham was then due up at 'Fortress Upton Park' and the
result would be a 12-point haul from four games. But, once
again, West Ham confounded everyone.*

BLAGG, Nov 2001

Lady Blagg has a saying that she likes to drop into the
conversation whenever I make a mistake (which is quite
often, as she will tell you). 'That'll larn ya' she says with a
slow nod of her glamorous head. (Well, she is a Geordie –
what do you expect?). How wise her words seemed this
weekend.

Your favourite Online columnist was pretty busy last week
and I barely had a moment free to get in here and crow
about the away win at Ipswich. No matter, I thought. I'll wait
till Monday and dovetail it nicely with the expected win over
Fulham and produce a rip-roaring, 'look how we're
improving/what a fine manager Glenn Roeder is turning out
to be' type of column. Will I ever bloody larn?

The annoying thing is that the away win over Ipswich was
a cracking game, a fine team performance with a superiority
which merited a score line more in keeping with that
provided by young Jermain Defoe before that late Ipswich
strike. By comparison, the Fulham game was a poor,
annoying, niggling type of affair that left a bad taste in the
mouth. I think I was just as annoyed and frustrated over
losing at home to the Cottagers as I was to getting thumped
by Blackburn.

BLAGG, today

*On and on it went. Frustrating defeat followed encouraging
win. Nobody was convinced that Glenn Roeder had it all
right but there were enough confident showings to suggest
he didn't have it all wrong either.*

*Major talking point, though, was the apparently
deteriorating relationship between manager and star player
and captain, Paolo Di Canio. The Italian maestro was never
an easy person to handle and Harry Redknapp had several*

amusing anecdotes about trying to cope with the player's mercurial talent. But it seemed as if, while Di Canio was happy to cross swords with Redknapp, his patience with Roeder was more strained.

Di Canio had gone into print with some outspoken criticisms of Roeder's appointment and his fellow club professionals. Chief among the Italian's gripes were accusations of lack of effort, a delicious irony as many fans felt that it was Di Canio's own lack of desire – particularly in away games where he seemed to drift through matches – that was the cause of the Hammers' hot and cold form. The real issues in this relationship were to come to the fore during Roeder's second season in charge. In the 2001-02 campaign, though, there was still enough wallpaper to cover the cracks and the fans were split on what Paolo was really doing for the side.

Interestingly though, Roeder was keen to promote harmony between himself and the feisty Italian during the first part of his tenure. Speaking to the Daily Telegraph's Henry Winter later in the season, Roeder spoke of his relationship with his Captain: "When I got the job some managers said to me 'Di Canio is unhandleable (sic)', but I haven't found him the monster everyone told me he would be. Paolo is so passionate about football and doing well. He knows how high my standards are. What drives Paolo mad is when players' standards do not match his."

These are interesting contradictions considering a lot of the press reports at the time. In that same interview the conundrum of the Redknapp–Roeder–Brown relationship is revealed.

"Of the 22-24 players in our squad, between six and eight are sub-Premiership standard. The players who came into the club after Rio Ferdinand were sold have fallen short of the class we want but, unfortunately, they are on three or four-year contracts. In terms of salary, we are paying top dollar and have been left holding several babies, all of them screaming.

"The board understand the squad situation. Probably that was what led to the downfall of Harry, because they could see the quality was not being brought in that should have been. If I can survive long enough, I can flush these players out of the club as their contracts run out."

This interview, given in December 2001, is a fascinating look at what was occurring at West Ham during this period, particularly as Roeder suggests that the dream job offered to Curbishley and McClaren was considered and rejected by both men almost certainly due to the poor standard of the players available to them, allied to the high salaries and long contracts that effectively tied them to the club in some sort of 'golden handcuffs'.

Roeder's suggestion that he was the only man left standing willing to take on the role may jar slightly with those whose opinion of Glenn's abilities are slightly less than flattering – but once again there is an palpable sense that somehow the average fan was denied knowledge of things that were happening behind the scenes.

A look at the web sites around this period reveals a surprising trend in hindsight, too. Support for Glenn Roeder was strong with belief that more money should have been made available for him to strengthen the team – particularly in defence - while support for Paolo Di Canio was mixed, with many feeling that his influence on the side as captain was disruptive and undermined Roeder's position.

Di Canio frequently made a great play of showing his support for Roeder, running to the touchline to celebrate with him when he scored a goal, but it wasn't unusual for that to be followed a week later with the Italian griping about some aspect of the club he disagreed with.

Against this backdrop it was pretty surprising tabloid news to find that, in late January following another disastrous away trip to Stamford Bridge where the Hammers lost 5-1, rumours began to surface that Manchester United boss Alex Ferguson had offered £2m for the services of the Hammers' Italian captain. Ferguson apparently viewed Di Canio's mercurial talent as a vital asset missing in his club's attempt to regain the Champions League trophy that they had held a year earlier.

Debate raged among Hammers fans as to whether or not Di Canio's sale would be a good thing for the club...

Bill, Sydney Oz

If Paolo leaves then I know what my memory of him will be: overrated. Other teams thought more of him than we

64

did. The good he did outranked his poor performance but not by a great amount.

We all know he shouldn't be taking every corner, throw-in or penalty kick and we all know that no-one at the club can stop him. Will Ferguson stop him if he joins Man U? What do you think?

Any Old Iron

Up until last week's Chelsea game I had been championing the case for Di Canio to stay. But after his pathetic performances at Stamford Bridge I really want Ferguson to take him off our hands now. Come on, Manure, up your bid now.

I don't think I've ever seen such a lack of REAL effort from a captain of our club in 40 years. It doesn't matter what he says, it's what he does that counts. I don't think it's worth the risk of keeping him any longer 'cos he might go into a big time sulk and be a complete liability.

AfM

I think we need to be careful about how we view offloading PDC. I've heard that the players think Paolo is a class act and they view selling Di Canio as a lack of ambition.

Scuffler

I don't think selling Paolo is a good thing at all. Have you all got short memories or something? The man is one of the best players ever to pull on the shirt. If he goes we'll look back at these days and wonder why the hell we did it. What I would say is that Glenn needs to be tougher with him – does he have to take every free kick and corner?

Gerald Irons

Remember the way he ran over to take the ball away from Joey Cole for that second half corner last week? You know I'd love to be in that dressing room. What do the players think of him? Would Joe have been pissed with him or would he think it's part of what PDC is all about, and you have to take the crunchie with the smooth, as Billy Bragg once said.

Duncan
Is that Billy Bragg or Billy Blagg?

Jayee
I think Blagg only writes the columns on WHO, I'm pretty sure he had nothing to do with 'New England' or 'The Man in the Iron Mask'.

Billy Blagg
Rest assured, Jayee and Duncan, if I'd written 'Levi Stubbs Tears' then I wouldn't be sitting here at 1am in the morning reading this!

PaulN
Several things will define Sir Glenn's campaign this year, and I think he'll have to show PDC that he, Roeder, is in charge. I would've loved seeing Di Canio get subbed for (Laurent) Courtois in the second half. I love Paolo but he's way out of line lately

Reality Check
I agree that the present situation is holding the club and team back – and that's what I can't understand in WH not accepting (United's) bid. In fairness to Di Canio, this must be effecting him as well as the team/club/manager in attitude, planning, etc. Therefore, for the life of me, I can't understand why they did not accept the first official bid and be done with it if, as seems likely, the club/manager really wants him out anyway. If we were talking about millions, I could understand it, but we are not. We need a replacement, though, as an injury to Defoe/Kanouté would leave us with, realistically, only (Paul) Kitson – a player who gets every injury and illness known to man. I fully expect him to cry off with bubonic plague next.

Any Old Iron
These last few games were too much to take from our captain and one of the most talented players ever to don the C&B. He has cheated himself and us. If I was boss I would have played (Ragnvald) Soma, and that would have been an improvement.

Gutted-Hammer
Paolo Going? Nooooooooooooooooooooooooooo...

Whufcroe
Well, hopefully the injuries are behind them now but I am in favour of waiting until the summer when we can rebuild the team to better effect.

In all honesty we are not in any relegation trouble and I would hope that we could get by with Defoe, Kanouté, Kitson, (Svetoslav) Todorov and (Richard) Garcia.

On the point about the players not liking Di Canio, we can only go on what others who are 'better placed' have told us, so it up to each of us to make our own minds up about him. I'm not sure Di Canio is as bad as some make him out to be and up until 18 months ago I loved to watch him. But IMHO this is what is holding this club back and his displays against Chelsea have just tipped me over the edge.

The Vulture
If you lot base your judgement of players on two performances rather than three seasons, all I can say is I'm glad none of you are managing West Ham United.

Jack flash
I'm getting sick and tired of the PDC speculation. Now or the end of the season, he's off – so what difference does a few months make?

If we can get £3.5m now, that would probably be a lot more than what we'd get at the end of the season. You can't blame the bloke for wanting one last big pay off and a crack at the big time in Europe, even if he may possibly be watching from the bench.

Kevin Isaac
I agree it is time to play without Di Canio. We can then have two strikers playing up front and Joe Cole will come into his own. We do not need a sulking captain who is not interested. I think we have seen the best of him and will only see rare flashes in the future.

Bignumbernine

The Guardian this morning said they believe that Man U and WHU have agreed a £2.5m fee but that Man U won't go ahead with the deal until Dwight Yorke is sold. They hinted Boro have cooled on that deal. Don't know if there is any truth in this.

Sanfranjef

I think Manure are waiting for Boro to agree terms with Dwight Yorke. So we're waiting for Yorke, too. Seems pathetic to me that WHU won't just buy whoever GR has lined up as replacement anyway. Why should we delay? If PDC doesn't go, then he wouldn't be first choice anymore at the moment. Kitson must be off in the summer, so we need another striker anyway.

FABIO

I'm 100 per cent behind Roeder. But the fact is, we will never know what his first choices are for a replacement and how far he has to go down his hit list 'till the board give their blessing. He needs our support and if the board thinks every fan is on their back there is more likelihood that he may get that little bit more cash that he needs to do a proper job.

What I do know is that Di Canio has been ineffective all season. Four goals from open play is a disgrace and he has taken that to another level over the past few weeks.

I don't think we need to replace Di Canio anyway right now. I would start with Kanouté and Defoe, with Kitson as back up. If we wanted a player to play in a game in the withdrawn role that Paolo seems to play, we could do worse than give Garcia a little run.

Telgee

Sell him now, please! He's been great but now it's time to go. Bring in that bloke (Bobby) Zamora and make sure we can hold onto Kanouté and Defoe. Paolo is part of our history now – let's all wake up to that fact.

Minty

They need to sign him by the cut-off date for Champions League registration and that's just two days off, so either way this saga will come to an end soon.

Hotplates Davis
How WHU is this? We get a legend playing for us and we can't wait to get shot of him? Man U want him and we go 'Yeah, that Ferguson's a mug – let him go to Old Trafford and we can go and buy some second division player who scored a hat-trick against Northampton last week'. How clever are we? Remember people said the florid-faced Scotsman was a fool to take a chance on that Frenchman from Leeds? Ferguson does not buy mugs and he knows he can get the best from Di Canio and the day he can't, then he'll let him go. That's why Man U are where they are and why we are where we are. Personally, I'd be asking questions about Roeder's management skills.

Simon.s
It's time to bring the Di Canio saga to a close. All good things come to an end. Take the money and get down to Brighton as quickly as possible and snap up Zamora before it's too late.

Flea Taxi
He will stay, he might even get a new contract, but his role will be radically redefined.

Anonny
AFM – I think you are well off the mark. It would seem that some players don't even want to pass to him now. His disruption of the club is a disgrace. He (Roeder) could have nipped it in the bud from day one but didn't. GR should get back on the phone this very minute and offer to take the £2.5 or even £1.5m. Let's get rid of him and let's start to move the club forward.

SD
How does it show a lack of ambition if we get rid of an ineffective, disruptive, fractious 33-year-old past his prime?

AfM
You've all got it wrong. I wanted him to go but I have since been convinced by players in the club that the rumours of

rifts between him and others are an overstatement, to say the least, and that if he goes it will signify a lack of ambition from the club.

For this reason alone, I want him to stay.

Cleatus

Trouble is, on the back of the last few weeks, who would want him?

Nels

Historically, I've seen influential players like Moore, Hurst and Brooking leave and, for a while, the team almost seems to play better. I think it's because, if you're in a hole, players will often pass to the man with a bit of magic and hope he can conjure something up. If he's not there, then they have to think differently. The problem is not what happens immediately after but what the club does futuristically to replace the outgoing player. I don't mind PDC going if we look to be bringing the next flawed genius in. But I can't see that at the moment. **** me – we haven't replaced Moore yet!

BLAGG, today

Courtois, Todorov, Kitson, Garcia – all surprising names suggested as the answer to Paolo Di Canio's wayward temperament. Even an early reference to Bobby Zamora who was to join the club from Spurs almost three years later as makeweight in the £7m Jermain Defoe deal. If that suggests turmoil in the minds of the fans, then it may go some way to explaining the corresponding confusion on the pitch.

To muddy the infuriating waters of the Hammers' inconsistency, Roeder's reign was occasionally disturbed by stories emanating from outside the club suggesting that all was not as it seems.

BLAGG, Dec 2001

Fans of the top-notch BBC series *The X Files* will know of the 'Deep Throat' character who regularly gives Mulder and Scully tips as to what is going on with the conspiracy theories and why. Critics of the show may suggest giving tips to viewers as to what is going on in the series may not be a bad idea either, but I digress.

West Ham Online – this modest, little website – has its own 'Deep Throat' (and please stop sniggering at the back there!) as Alex and I regularly receive emails from a mysterious man who tips the wink about the latest developments at Upton Park. Most of this stuff is libellous, unprintable and often unprovable.

And in true *X-Files* style, Alex and I have no idea if we are being given misinformation to throw us off the track of what is really happening. Short of contacting the Paranoia Society (motto: If you think people are talking about you, It's because they probably are), my intrepid editor and I can do nothing more than tap our noses in a conspiratorial way and reveal what we can as we see fit.

I mention this because most of my time this week has been spent watching the appalling spectacle of our ex-manager and current chairman fighting it out and who decided to sell 'you know who' to 'you know what team' in a tell-tale 'exclusive' in a national paper this week. Some of the rumours laid bear there are things that have been fed to the Online team over the last few months.

For those who missed any of the stories flying around, the whole sorry story began in the *Daily Mail* with a serialisation of a book that purports to expose the corruption prevalent in football. Some fans on this site got a bit sniffy because It was the Fascist Appeaser that ran the story but, truth to tell, the extracts were from a book by Tom Bower, entitled *Broken Dreams*, and, to my knowledge, that has nothing to do with the *Mail* other than they printed an extract from it.

The book, subtitled *Vanity, Greed and the Souring of British Football*, examines several big transfer deals in recent times and attempts to find out what happened to the money being paid and the involvement of various interested parties. And guess what transfer comes under the spotlight?

Investigating the sale of Rio Ferdinand to Leeds United, the first instalment of the tale indicated that Terence Brown had not wanted Rio to be sold and the chairman was astonished when Harry suggested that it would be a good move for the club and for the player's future development. Things then get a bit murky with odd tales of £300,000 incentives being offered to Harry to 'not spend the Rio money' while Terence Brown is portrayed as a man throwing cash at a problem while doubting the sanity of those spending it. Admitting he was not a 'football man', Brown appears as an honourable person trying to pin a tail on an ever-revolving donkey.

From my jaundiced view, the idea of a chairman offering a manger a large amount of dosh not to spend an even larger amount of dosh is, frankly, difficult to believe. Why just not give him the money to spend? Presumably, Harry didn't have his own signature on the cheque book (although at this club nothing would surprise me!). Still, the first part of the serialisation did enough to make Brown look like a man who had been sold short as he searched, scratching his head, trying to make sense of where his millions were going and why H thought it good business to pay £1.2m for Gary Charles, only to dump him three weeks later with a shrug of the shoulders and a 'what do you expect for that type of money' comment.

The high salaries thrown at useless 'free' signings and the odd idea of having mega-earning Davor Suker sitting on our bench when, according to H 18 months previously, he would walk into any club's first team, is a worrying example of the type of shenanigans that make little sense to us on the outside.

My good friend Paul took the time to ring me after the first part of the story to say that our Tel had come out of it looking particularly shiny. Of course, it couldn't last, and Sunday's revelations that – according to 'other sources' - Mr B had been slightly shy of the truth just made the whole thing even more impossible to judge objectively. This time Harry claimed the £300,000 gift was a thank you from the club (truth or not, it sounds more plausible) with the even more worrying tale that our Rio had even been offered 'golden handshake' money to move to Leeds when he really didn't want to leave.

More damaging accusations fly with thinly veiled stories about the board asset-stripping the club while boosting Glenn Roeder's profile to make his appointment appear more acceptable to the fans (yeah, right!).

In truth, nobody comes out of this well (apart from the poor fans – but we don't count, of course) but what really concerned me was the shocking realisation that the stories told by this pair were so obviously different that, quite simply, one of them must be lying through his teeth. I suspect most of us will side with Harry over Terence Brown but, in truth, would you buy a used car from Redknapp & Sons?

Harry probably has the will of the people on his side but, sadly, it doesn't mean he is telling the truth. If it were to be found that it was his idea to sell Rio so that he could invest some cash in some, frankly dodgy, MOT failed, Liverpool players to whom his son was acting as an agent, then West Ham's current plight could be laid at his door as much as Mr B's or Genial Glenny Boy's.

I have no idea who is telling the truth but I do know that the whole thing stinks and it only seems to confirm various rumours that Alex and myself have encountered over the past two years that suggest Hammers fans have been done over like a kipper on the state of this club.

I've said before and I'll say again: Terence Brown's silence does him and the board no justice and the sooner our chairman decides to make a stand (preferably one that doesn't cost £18m) and tell us exactly what is going on at Upton Park, the better we will all be for it.

BLAGG, today

As the Pet Shop Boys once remarked, nothing has been proved.

While past shenanigans were being mulled over and before the alleged bid by Manchester United for Di Canio, Glenn Roeder had been quietly strengthening the team. Czech international defender Tomas Repka arrived via Fiorentina of Italy, ex-Hammer Don Hutchison returned from influential spells at Everton and Sunderland as a regular Scottish international but, more importantly, a bold statement had been made by the manager in typically understated Roeder style.

Coup of the season was the fantastic light fandango played by the new boss when he purchased David James from Aston Villa. Eyebrows were raised when the signing was announced: "Why do we need a goalkeeper?" the fans all asked. The then No. 1, Shaka Hislop, was sound enough, wasn't he? Wouldn't the £3m be better spent elsewhere?

The manager then pointed out the obvious fact that we had all missed. David James was an England international and when was the last time West Ham purchased a current England player? Suddenly, James moved from being Aston Villa's suspect heir to the yellow jersey to being considered a cert for the England squad from the off. Later to replace retiring England stopper David Seaman after the World Cup that summer, the signing of James showed a sleight of hand that would have amazed even David Blaine.

With James seemingly steadying the defence and hope for Repka's influence when he came to terms with English referees, West Ham's paradox of a season suddenly peaked. Just before Christmas 2001 came the result that gave Roeder's season the impetus he must have prayed for. A 1-0 win over Manchester United at Old Trafford with a superbly taken headed goal by Jermain Defoe meant that talk of relegation could already be banished and whispered conversations about European qualification could now be granted.

Redknapp had, of course, won 1-0 at Old Trafford in the FA Cup during the previous season so the Premiership win formed, in the fans' minds at least, a kind of unique double. It also marked a high point in Roeder's stewardship at the club. For a while all the doubters had to back-off as they conceded that, at his first attempt, Roeder had achieved something other managers worked seasons for or never managed to achieve.

Sadly, my own memories of that day are clouded by the fact that, lured by some ridiculous odds being quoted by local Turf Accountant, Ronnie Dubious, I visited the bookies on the morning of the match ready to put a fiver on Defoe to score first in a 1-0 win. But a huge queue inside, and pressure from Lady B to go Christmas shopping, meant the bet was never placed. The gambling money was later invested on a Starbuck's Eggnog Latte.

On such things have empires fallen.

BLAGG, Dec 2001

For anyone wishing to meet me, I will be outside the Lower Bobby on Saturday, bending over with a sign saying 'Kick

Me' strapped to my back. Feel free to take a pot shot!

Almost as bad as the loss of a large deposit in the Blagger's bank account is the fact that my reaction to Jermain's strike against the loathsome Mancs wasn't the usual: "Get in there, my son" air-punching scream that normally accompanies any Saturday afternoon on the car radio but instead was a low moan of "Nooooo....." I feel quite guilty about that now so I would just like to record here how proud I am that West Ham have defeated the awful Infidels twice in the same calendar year. Well done, lads!

The usual drill on any defeat of Man U is to briefly praise the opposition and then drone on about how the Mancs have done this or failed to do that. Frankly, I'm peed off with it and I think it must be mentioned that West Ham were worthy winners on Saturday and Man U got exactly what they deserved. Results like Saturday's simply can't come often enough.

Dee Hammer

BEST NEWS IN A LONG TIME! Who saw those three points coming, then? Well done to Glenn and the lads for a quality victory for the Irons – different class. If a bit of a boost is what we needed to get us going this season, then I think we got one.

Fizz

Great win, more of the same please. I see the *Sunday Mirror* gave Keane MOTM. What the **** is going on when a player who should have been sent off, abuses the ref and gets out-played by two 20-year-olds is made MOTM?

Dibersdownunder

I remember asking, when we bought David James, why we needed to buy him when we already have two good goalkeepers? I now have to eat my words and say that since he has played for the Hammers, especially against Man U, he has been magnificent. He would have to be called a world-class keeper. The difference between James and Hislop is very wide.

Vhammer

How can Rodeo be pleased with such a poor result against such weak opponents? Sack him for this performance alone. If you can't beat second-rate teams like this by at least three goals, you don't deserve to be in the Premiership.

Earl of Wakefielder
More Man U-baiting for you:

Did you hear that the Post Office has had to recall their latest stamps? They had pictures of Man Utd players on them. People couldn't figure out which side to spit on.

Did you hear about the politician who was found dead in a Man Utd shirt? The police had to dress him up in women's underwear in order to save his family from the embarrassment.

Four surgeons are taking a coffee break. The first one says: "Accountants are the best to operate on because when you open them up everything inside them is numbered." The second surgeon says: "Nah, librarians are the best; everything inside them is in alphabetical order." Third surgeon says: "Try electricians. Everything inside them is colour-coded." The fourth one pipes up: "I prefer Man Utd fans. They're heartless, spineless and gutless and their heads and arses are interchangeable."

Q. You're trapped in a room with a tiger, a rattlesnake and a Man Utd fan. You have a gun with two bullets. What do you do? A. Shoot the Man Utd fan – twice.

Q. What's the difference between Man Utd and a jet engine? A. A jet engine eventually stops whining.

Q. How many Man Utd fans does it take to change a light bulb? A. Seven – one to change it, five to moan about it and the manager to say that if the referee had done his job in the first place, the light bulb would never have gone out.

BLAGG, today
In the second half of the 2001-02 season West Ham's form remained patchy but now included several victories that could be said to have been 'eked out'. These were the type of games that normally look like goalless draws after 15 minutes or matches where the Hammers may well have gone down to a late winner in previous seasons. Two games

towards the end of the season – both 1-0 wins against Everton and Middlesbrough – were good examples of games where little could be said of the style of play but much could be made of the points gained.

The Premiership mid-table was a morass of clubs too good to go down but not good enough to challenge for Europe. A huge points gap had opened up between sixth and seventh place and there was a real feeling that the Premiership was now effectively two divisions rolled into one. Still, at least West Ham could now claim to be top of the 'other' division because, as the season ended, Roeder's side finished in a very creditable seventh place.

Had the team over-achieved? After all, a few points dropped here or there would have seen them just above the relegation pack. Or was Roeder gradually turning the side into the team we all thought they should be? Some new faces had joined the club – most notably England goalkeeper David James – but, unfortunately, history would not be kind to the manager on this aspect of his tenureship.

Perhaps one of the more unfortunate assumptions of Roeder's reign is that the £11m received from Chelsea for Frank Lampard was somehow wasted in the same way that the Rio money had been squandered on the likes of Song and Camara.

In fact, some of the players who had joined the club had made a serious impact. Harry tried and tested Sebastian Schemmel before sending him back to France. Glenn Roeder brought him back for around £400,000 and by season's end the Frenchman was voted Hammer of the Year.

James represented, for the first time since Rio, a player who could raise the profile of the club. Often the 'face' to be seen in TV interviews or glossy magazines, James would be sought out for his views on fashion as well as football.

Tomas Repka, although not always the steadying influence the fans had hoped he would be given his Serie A experience, had turned into a favourite due to his aggressive, all-action persona. Repka's central defensive partnership with the unfairly, much-maligned Redknapp acquisition Christian Dailly was fitful but, on a good day, looked as if it certainly adequate enough for a reasonable Premiership side.

But unfortunately the transfer market was in loony tune mode in 2001-02 and within 12 months it was hard to make any sense of some of the figures paid for players that season. West Ham weren't the worst to suffer but it seems incredible now to think that Don Hutchison joined West Ham from Sunderland for £5m – eventually proving to be only worth a £1m or so less than Joe Cole when he eventually moved to Chelsea just under two years later.

Similarly, £5m seemed an enormous amount to pay for the erratic Repka. Although the defender's style still has its fans at Upton Park, the early months were hard on the Czech as he failed to come to terms with Premiership referees who handed him red cards seemingly at will.

But this must be viewed with the benefit of hindsight. With James, Trevor Sinclair and Cole all being named in England's World Cup squad for Japan/Korea 2002, there was little debate over the state of West Ham as they approached the 2002-03 season. The addition of a top class central defender and a full-back would seem to be all the squad required to push them into European contention.

Nothing could prepare the fans for what was about to transpire.

Chapter 6

DOWN AND OUT
Season 2002-03

West Ham approached the 2002-03 season with good reason to be confident. Seventh place the previous season had suggested that Glenn Roeder had managed to pull something off, although it has to be said not everyone was sure exactly what that was.

Unfortunately, at the time few realised that the Upton Park postman had seemingly run off with the cheque from the FA that had been awarded for the Hammers' seventh place finish. How else can you explain the chronic lack of funds available at that time? If there was a better explanation, then most fans seemed to have missed it.

The manager had spent a good deal of money on David James, Tomas Repka and Don Hutchison but there was strong belief that the defence desperately needed strengthening and the lack of two full-backs and a central defender were ultimately to prove crucial.

The difficulties in discussing the trauma of the 2002-03 season lie in the fact that hindsight lends an amazing lucidity to what was to transpire over the following 12 months. For example, it would be easy to talk about 'loss of form' but in some cases it amounted to more than that. In the case of at least two players, the summer of 2002 could be considered the pinnacle of their careers from which they would collapse in an embarrassing and undignified heap.

Who could have guessed the staggering loss of form that saw French wing-back Sebastian Schemmel go from the previous season's Hammer of the Year to lost soul within six months? By Christmas, the Frenchman was thought to have been shacked up with Lord Lucan and Shergar somewhere in South America with his Hammers career in tatters.

The World Cup, rather than acting as a fresh impetus to Trevor Sinclair, had taken its toll. Considered a regular England international as the season began, he became a shadow of his former self. In July and August 2002, there were rumours that Liverpool were considering a £12m offer for the popular ex-QPR man; but fans were, not unreasonably, adamant that the Hammers needed to hang onto their England internationals if they were to prove a force in the Premiership.

In similar, but rather stranger fashion, Glenn Roeder managed to acquire the free transfer services of Coventry City's Gary Breen, who had been outstanding for the Republic of Ireland in Korea and Japan. This looked a fantastic piece of business except for the fact that centre-back Breen never again scaled the heights that he managed in the Far East. So Roeder, rather unfairly, got the stick for poor judgement on a player who should have really been quite good enough to have plugged at least one of the gaps in the Hammers' rearguard.

Dovetailing with all these factors was the virtual collapse of the transfer market. It wasn't a collapse that was dramatic and easily heralded but rather a slow decline that almost crept up unawares. Sometimes it all looks so obvious in hindsight. While sifting through the fan comments left on WHO at this time, there was a post contradicting most of the views of the time, claiming that West Ham should cash in on Trevor Sinclair's success at the 2002 World Cup and went on to suggest five or six players who could be purchased with the available cash.

Fluctuating player fortunes and changing attitudes make the post irrelevant now but it is staggering to think how the sale of one of the crown jewels in July 2002 could have possibly rebuilt the whole side within nine months. Twelve months later and a sixth of the alleged fee offered by Liverpool was all it took to prise the popular winger away to Manchester City – and many Man City fans feel their club was ripped off!

Many teams suffered from this collapse, of course, but the Hammers could rightly curse the fact that the £11m received from Chelsea for Frank Lampard was spent on just two players when, barely a year later, it could have rebuilt the entire first team. (Anybody who suggests that they knew that Frank Lampard would be worth nearly twice the value of Joe Cole is not to be trusted.)

Almost as important as the effect on the market itself, though, was the new transfer window. Like many ideas the transfer window was thought to have been a benefit to those less fortunate; the theory being that the larger clubs had to cope with the squads they had, barring an available transfer period at the start and middle of the season, bringing them into line with the smaller, less well-off clubs.

In fact, what happened was the bigger clubs simply bought everyone they thought they may need – top players being strangely happy to sit on the bench for a European tie – while the smaller clubs hoped and prayed that nobody in their squad became injured.

Inevitably, the biggest losers in the transfer window where the fans who were denied the opportunity to see a transfer made that could transform their team's season. Memories of the type of impact made by the Hartson/Kitson transfer during Harry's reign, that turned a relegation season in 1997 into a successfully stirring battle against the odds, were now a thing of the past. If your team were woeful in late summer and autumn, then the only respite could now be gained during a frantic rush in January.

If this was the backdrop against which the 02-03 campaign was played out then it can often be forgotten how some of us approached the forthcoming season with some optimism.

BLAGG, Aug 2002

The fact is it's not only the players who are quietly confident. I've seen few doubters hanging around the Online cyberspace and that must be a first. In fact, everywhere there's a kind of buzz that this year maybe – just maybe – West Ham can pull off something a little spectacular.

The main reason for this is the growing stature of manager Glenn Roeder. Who would have thought we would all be standing here, almost a year after he was appointed, discussing what a good boss he is? But Roeder's quiet, confident way of going about things is starting to impress a lot of people. The players obviously rate him highly, the fans have taken to him and all we need now is that extra bit of something to propel us forward.

And that extra something? In my view, it's just plain and simple good luck. The kind of luck that means we don't play too many games without injured players. The kind of luck that means we don't have to travel to Anfield in the third round of the FA Cup – that type of thing. After all, we're due some luck, aren't we?

For me, our season rests on Roeder sorting out the perennial nightmare of the West Ham awayday. Ever since I was a boy I've travelled to away games with hope more than expectation but to make a real fist of a challenge for a European place we must ensure that the defeats column in the away section doesn't contain double figures. It's a tall challenge – history isn't with us on this one – but I think Roeder is a man tactically astute enough to achieve it.

Nevertheless, I'm bullish about our prospects this season and I hope my faith isn't misplaced. The ground looks good, the players look strong, the manager appears to know what he's doing; surely this must be a big year for us? I know we are West Ham United and anything is possible – but we can turn those dreams into reality for once, can't we?

BLAGG, today

One match later and it was a 4-0 opening day defeat at Newcastle. Things looked grim already.

But then came the 'What if?' match. In only the second game of the season, and the first at 'Fortress Upton Park', West Ham played superbly against local rivals Arsenal and were comfortably 2-1 up when the home side were justly awarded a penalty. Fredi Kanouté stepped up to take the kick but, instead, played a virtual backpass to Arsenal keeper David Seaman, so the scoreline that never was went begging. Arsenal seemed to find a second wind that wasn't there previously and pulled back to 2-2 with a late Wiltord strike.

A draw was disappointing after having the opportunity of going three-one up, of course. But most people leaving the ground that August day just spoke excitedly about the showing against the Premiership's top team.

Who could have imagined that it would be the following January before West Ham would win at home?

Two home defeats, against Charlton Athletic and West Bromwich Albion, suggested that something was not right somewhere and the usual away-day defeat at Tottenham, followed by a lacklustre draw at home to Manchester City, suggested a chilly autumn lay ahead.

But then, at the end of September, a 3-2 Paolo Di Canio-inspired win at Stamford Bridge suggested that, as the pundits always tell us, the Premiership is a marathon not a sprint and all was not lost. Despite another home shocker against Birmingham City, another two away wins against Sunderland and Fulham pushed the Hammers just above the relegation zone. Sadly, it was to be the last time that the Hammers faithful could feel comfortable.

The litany of defeats during the following months of the 2002-03 season make depressing reading. What really hurt the fans, though, was the complete lack of anything approaching form, skill or confidence on the Upton Park pitch. Most fans expected to drop points away but at home the side lost in embarrassing circumstances to sides like Southampton, Everton and Leeds United – teams who were all struggling themselves. Every week the faithful turned up expecting it would be the week that the first home win would be achieved, yet every week they went home disappointed.

Even now it seems incredible to imagine that any side could go so long without a home win, particularly as the board kept faith with their beleaguered manager during the whole of that time.

There was barely a lone voice who thought that Glenn Roeder should have kept his job after the embarrassing 3-4 home defeat by Leeds in November. Even that lone voice had been strangled and buried under the patio by the time the team lost 4-1 at Aston Villa later in the month.

On a personal level, due to...er...'seasonal fluctuations in the job market' (where were Jobserve when I needed them?) the Blagg column began being posted from very exotic places.

BLAGG, Nov 2002

Dublin has loomed large in my life this week. Two days (soon to become three) with Lady Blagg in the Republic's capital last weekend, followed by a goal and a sterling performance from Dion this weekend. Life follows such symmetry at times, doesn't it?

For someone making tentative steps from a failed career in Information Technology to a new one in freelance writing, Dublin isn't exactly the place to inspire your confidence. You might think your writing skills are coming on awfully well and then you read a few well-chosen phrases from Samuel Beckett, James Joyce and Oscar Wilde and you suddenly realise that the postman's job might be a better bet after all.

Before last Sunday, I had imagined that I might catch the Manchester United game on a pub TV screen and be able to cheer on the claret and blue, surrounded by a bunch of jovial Irishmen supporting the Mancs. In fact, I gave up fairly early on trying to find a bar showing the game and elected instead to tread in the footsteps of Brendan Behan on a literary tour of the city. Several Jamesons and Guinness' later, I had almost forgotten that we had even played.

In fact, it was only due to thick fog at Stansted, causing the cancellation of all flights out of Dublin on Monday night, that I caught the match at all. Lounging in luxury in an airport hotel, courtesy of the insurance company, I watched *The Premiership* highlights show and saw the two offside goals for the first time. I was satisfied – if not exactly pleased – with a draw and slightly encouraged by the stories that insisted we had looked a half-decent side.

For the rest of the week, though, I have felt as if I was trapped in the Hans Christian Andersen story about the king's new clothes. Everywhere I looked people were talking about us having 'turned the corner', with the Man U result being seen as a springboard for the rest of the season. Even the redoubtable Alex – with whom I seldom differ – seemed to see some spark of life in the corpse of our Premiership squad. I hadn't been part of the atmosphere surrounding the game, so I decided to keep quiet even though my thoughts on the corpse had more in keeping with those of Prof. Günter von Hagen.

Even so, I was devastated by the result at Villa Park. I'm

always happy to be proved wrong, so I get no pleasure from the outcome, but I actually think a result that drops us to the bottom of the table, when the side below us has lost as well, just about plumbs new depths. Four-one is a hammering and, coming at a place like Villa Park where I really thought we might get a result, just about tops it off. That Dion Dublin – an ageing striker packed off to Millwall last season on a last hurrah – found it so easy to torment our defence is little short of embarrassing.

But what more can we say? Is there any facet of the club that we haven't discussed over the past four months? What other ideas can anyone come up with? In some ways, I feel that I should just ditch the current situation and write a couple of columns about the players with the funniest haircuts or the best players we've ever seen – things which I have done quite happily in the past. But then I feel as if I'm not taking the situation seriously.

Anyway, I don't think we are in any doubt at all that next week's game against Southampton is a must-win affair. Personally, I think Glenn will fall on his sword if we don't get a win then. Beyond that, though, we're obviously in a dogfight until the end of the season. Our first priority must be to get off the bottom by Christmas and then wait for the January sales.

All of which brings me nicely back to the written word again. Last week, on one of the message boards, someone pointed out a simple truth that we all know to hold true but, to see it actually written, made it all the more relevant.

The comment was simple: What large business wouldn't pay out £10m in order to ensure that they don't lose £30m? I'm not sure it was James Joyce who wrote it but it will do for me as a literary statement for the week.

BLAGG, today

The Southampton game was another desperate affair that West Ham could, and should, have won, and then, with minutes to spare and a goalless draw looking likely, ended up as another horrendous home defeat.

Christmas approached and it was time for 'colour by numbers' headlines. 'Since the inception of the Premiership no team has stayed up that has been bottom on Christmas

Day' cooed the pundits in sharp suits and dodgy ties. In fact, there are a number of clubs who have survived this alarming statistic but they had the good grace do it when the top league was called Division One.

However, in a staggering rewrite of history that even Pol Pot would have blanched at, this statistic had been erased in 'Year Zero' when the Premiership began, barely a decade earlier. Whatever the historical facts, though, there was no doubt that the Hammers' remaining results at home were crucial and they were severely dented when Bolton Wanderers managed a 1-1 draw at Upton Park on December 21 to ensure the home club occupied the deadly bottom spot just days before Santa was due to arrive.

From August to December West Ham United had not won a single game in front of the Upton Park faithful.

But then the dawning of a new year and the opening of the transfer window brought new hope – of sorts. In from Spurs came Les Ferdinand, a player deemed too old when West Ham had contemplated purchasing him two seasons before; Rufus Brevett's arrival from Fulham brought the cover we desperately needed for the ageing Nigel Winterburn at left-back; and finally, under cover of dark clouds and the rumble of thunder, there was the arrival of 'Bad Boy' Lee Bowyer.

The spikey midfielder's transfer from Leeds United for a nominal fee provoked controversy among fans.

BLAGG, Jan 2003

Regular readers will know that Blagg Acres hasn't seen a decent pay cheque since Brazil carried off the World Cup last summer so, with the offer of some work, a hot meal and a bed in a far-flung northern town, this week's column comes courtesy of a lonely hotel room in windy Durham. Next week it's Leeds and the following week Birkenhead. It's all gravy when you're a roving correspondent for Online.

So, with the wind whistling underneath the hotel door, the laptop plugged in and the absence of any type of 'Adult' channel on the TV, what better time to turn my reluctant thoughts to the vexing question of Lee Bowyer.

Now before you all groan and pull up another page, let me say that I tackle the thorny subject only because it's one of the major issues to affect West Ham in recent times and for me to ignore it would be a dereliction of my duty. Having said that, I wouldn't want you to think that I don't care about the matter or have strong opinions on it. On the contrary. It's just that it's difficult to tackle the subject in any way that hasn't already been covered in the thousands of words printed in other areas of the media. Still, I'm nothing if not a trier so, working on the usual Blagg maxim of playing Devil's Advocate, and setting more questions than I answer, here goes.

First up on a personal level, I'm very uncomfortable about the signing of Lee Bowyer. I don't hold with the spurious argument that the man was found not guilty in the recent Leeds court case and he has been further tarred with unproven comments from an ex-girlfriend. Frankly, if you chuck enough dark stuff then some of it will stick. I think Lee Bowyer is fairly covered in it.

Now although I consider that I have strong political opinions, I've never been a member of any party and tend to shy away from the type of political debate that usually develop in pubs and the back of taxis. Nevertheless, I loathe racism and the only political rally I have ever attended in my life was in support of the Anti-Nazi league. Nazi and racism are synonymous words in my dictionary and history teaches us that racism – be it in the guise 'ethnic cleansing' or 'lebensraum' – is responsible for most of the ills of mankind

But what has this to do with football? Well, in some respects, nothing. Lee Bowyer is a top quality footballer that has been signed for next to nothing with the sole intention of helping West Ham United stay in the Premiership. From that angle he has been an excellent signing. Sure, he comes with some well-documented baggage but is his crime that it is well documented? For example, I have no idea if Paolo Di Canio has strong right-wing beliefs. He doesn't threaten to beat up Pakistanis so I assume not (although there are stories that he was part of an ultra right-wing group in his younger days) but, as a fan, I know nothing beyond what the player wants me to know.

Bowyer seems to be in that hard battling, tenacious, 'wear your heart on your sleeve' type mould along with Roy Keane and others. It's difficult for them to hide and their volatile nature often spills over into their private lives. Subsequently, it's difficult to like them as people – and that's putting it mildly – but they seem to make excellent footballers. Is that a good enough reason to sign a player with a disreputable past? You'll probably have to ask me at the end of the season.

But the fact is that any player now plying his trade is going to have to share team space with a black or foreign player and I find it hard to reconcile a dislike of other races with the profession of professional footballer.

So what of the club's position? I have seen suggestions that West Ham have somehow betrayed the local community with the Bowyer signing – but I don't buy that. It has to be said that there are cultural differences that seem to indicate that football isn't a priority for most people of Asian descent. Nothing wrong with that – it's also unlikely that you would find a cricket crowd at Lord's rioting. That's just the way it is.

But looking at it further, can anyone accuse West Ham of betraying anyone of a different colour? I find this preposterous. This is the club that virtually dictated that black players were the equal of white players. We had three black players representing our club in the early 70s before anyone else even had one! I am proud of West Ham's integration of ethnic players, particularly in a geographical location and at a time when the repercussions could have been severe.

This has to be borne in mind when, as happened at the weekend, certain 'quality' newspapers start bringing up the infamous banana-throwing incidents of the distant past. Now, let's make it clear again, I hate racism and this type of incident is repugnant. However, certain fans also used to throw Mars bars at Paul Gascoigne and referees are always universally bald and blind. If footballers were allowed to wear spectacles then they would certainly be labelled as 'useless four eyed ****' whenever they missed an open goal. This doesn't make it right – but it does make it bloody confusing.

After all, we had black players in our own team at the time (a point a lot of papers playing the race card seem to miss). It's almost as if the banana-throwers thought our own black players were immune to the slur being heaped on the opposition. Is this likely? It seems bizarre to anyone with a couple of brain cells to rub together but why else is it OK to taunt other teams' black players while cheering your own? I didn't understand it then and I don't understand it now unless you put it down to blind stupidity – and perhaps that's more of an issue here than any other aspect.

It echoes to that time in the 70s when racist skinheads used to abuse blacks while happily listening to reggae. Later, as the black culture became 'cool', the racial aspect became disassociated from youth culture and, therefore, football violence. I've noticed, though, that when the media discuss racism they tend to lump all ethnic groups together as 'black' or 'coloured'. In fact, I've a feeling there is more than a touch of anti-Asian feeling rather than all-encompassing racism in Bowyer. This would, of course, make the supportive comments of Jermain Defoe superfluous.

The other mystery from my point of view is with regards to the media reaction. Why is it that the signing of Bowyer has bothered a lot of people while his previous incarnation with Leeds seems have been acceptable? When the player was under threat of jail, yet playing a blinder in Europe, most of the press merely contented themselves with discussing his football form against his personal turmoil. Why were they not as vociferous when the midfielder was turning out for the Elland Road side? Why were there no reports of how the Yorkshire club were 'betraying' their black or Asian community?

As ever with the printed media there is an uncomfortable feeling of double standards and headline-making to consider. As Bowyer is joining a club with an excellent record in the development of black players, perhaps it should be seen that West Ham are attempting to turn a 'wrong 'un'. Certainly, I believe Glenn Roeder should be commended for his attempts to get the new signing to take part in some local ethnic community work. In fact, I think this is essential if Lee Bowyer is ever to overcome his murky past.

Conversely, though, denying the racist and thuggish element is equally dangerous. I was appalled at the abuse metered out to the woman protesting at the front gate last Saturday. By all means disagree and feel free to make your points strongly. After all, it's your right. But there was a nasty taste left in the mouth watching the woman protester being verbally abused, having her banner torn down and having to suffer eyeball-to-eyeball confrontation. Taunts of 'lesbian' (eh?) and 'ugly *****' suggest that there are still a lot of worrying people out there.

These are the people that the *News of the World* saw on Saturday and it makes it difficult to defend our club when you see that type of reaction. The problem, though, is wider – much wider – and has to be taken in context to an overall lessening of tolerance in our society and a general rise in aggressive and boorish behaviour. Over Christmas I personally witnessed racial abuse handed out to an Asian petrol station attendant – by a man of West Indian descent. The anger and ferocity of his attack just left me stunned with just one thought in mind. Why? Why can someone get so angry with another human being for something that was (in this case) so petty? Of course, if I knew the answer to that I wouldn't be sitting here writing this for nothing!

So there are my thoughts on the matter. Not a good signing, morally, but I'm hardly stupid enough not to understand that the addition of Lee Bowyer to West Ham's books was one based purely on football. In those terms, perhaps Bowyer is worth a second chance if the management take the opportunity to try and reshape his outlook and character – or suffer the consequences if it doesn't pan out.

As to the wider issues, the signing has produced a lot of worrying signs and has shown some ugly characteristics in people attending matches at Upton Park, while once more revealing the media has again tried to gain the moral high ground by dragging itself in the gutter.

Whatever the outcome, Lee Bowyer is now a West Ham player and everyone connected to the club will be watching him to make sure that he doesn't kick our name into the mud. He has much to be ashamed of in his career so far, so let's hope he can make himself into a player and a person that we can be proud of.

Mind you, if one of the Sunday's are to be believed, Bowyer could be leaving us for Spurs in the summer regardless of whether he helps keep us up or not. Spurs?

Now that's something to think about, isn't it?

BLAGG, today

*While controversy reigned the new year heralded a shock
result. On January 29, 2003 – a statistic that will surely still
make shock reading a decade or more from now, Blackburn
Rovers became the first team to actually lose a match on the
Boleyn Ground turf during the 2002-03 season.*

*Despite that win, West Ham were now in a tailspin. It was
difficult to decide who was a good player going through a
bad patch, who simply didn't care, who had completely lost
it, what the manager could do about it all or even, in fact, if
he was capable of doing anything about it at all.*

*Glenn Roeder obviously bore the brunt of the criticism but
it was sometimes hard not to pity the man as he stood on
the touchline at every game, arms crossed and shielded by
his black leather jacket, seemingly willing the ball into the
opponents' net. Roeder remained stoical and upbeat despite
the perilous position and he never shirked the after-match
interview or the barbed criticism. The bottom line, though,
was that the manager had many experienced Premiership
and international players at his disposal and yet each week
the team had the look of a Wanstead Flats pub side on a
Sunday morning. The only difference being a pub side would
probably be better organised.*

*Many fans were obviously, and understandably, critical of
the manager and his tactics but many more turned instead
on chairman Terence Brown, likening the chairman and
manager's situation to that of a parent who gave his child a
loaded gun to play with and then seemed surprised when
the youngster used the weapon to shoot the cat.*

*Old questions about just what the chairman was doing
when he sacked Redknapp were re-opened, particularly now
that originally sought-after bosses Steve McClaren and Alan
Curbishley were doing well at Middlesbrough and Charlton.*

*Following another away defeat against and former 'small
club' Charlton Athletic, the Blagg column continued to post
more grim thoughts from far-flung corners of England*

BLAGG, Jan 2003

Now, I'm starting to understand how Alistair Cook must
have felt. Of course, the old radio and newspaper stalwart

was always lucky enough to send a 'Letter from America', and I suspect that there is nowhere as grim in the 'good ole US of A' as the rat hole from which I send this week's column. Still, I like to give these little weekly chats a bit of a leg-up and so, without further ado, I'd like to welcome you all to the pleasure dome that is . . . Birkenhead.

Now Birkenhead is without doubt the most depressing, decrepit, dilapidated, dingy, dung-heap of a dump it has ever been my misfortune to chance upon. On a good day – when the smog clears and the smell of molasses lifts – it's possible to see the Liver building across the Mersey and it makes you yearn for Scouseland. Liverpool is Nirvana compared to this place.

My mood was black enough anyway but it darkened even further when I found that, with no radio, a dead mobile, a long, grim walk to the nearest telephone kiosk and a TV with no Teletext that insists on only reporting local teams, I had no way of finding out the Charlton result until Thursday morning's newspapers. But was I better off not knowing? I think so.

The fat lady may not have sung yet but she's sure as hell mounting the podium and gargling hard. I found a 4-2 defeat at the hands of our 'little' South London neighbours pretty hard to stomach. For the umpteenth week running I really thought we would win. But now I can't see where our next point is going to come from.

I was chatting to a West Brom supporter today and even they have got us down as relegation certs and are looking to see who else they can consign to the dustbin to stay up themselves. We're worse than West Brom? I was going to say we've reached rock bottom but the Premiership table tells me that anyway.

Following Sunday's reversal at Highbury, this column was going to be used to fire off at the officials who seem to continually side with the major players. I still can't figure how – in a country where the underdog is always fancied – football referees still favour the big boys when they have enough of an advantage anyway. But, appalling as these decisions are, even I have to admit it looks as if we are bleating and I don't have the stomach to discuss how we can bring ourselves up to the playing level of Arsenal currently. I'd be happy to match Dagenham and Redbridge at the moment.

So what do we do? During WHO's long break before Christmas many people emailed me to ask if I would come in guns blazing on the 'Brown Out' and 'Is Glenn Roeder Worth a Carrot?' issues and, so far, I have steadfastly refused to be drawn beyond what I have said previously. My feelings about this are well documented. I'm all for replacing something that doesn't work but what do we replace it with?

I realise this is mainly down to age and experience but it's only fair to warn those protesting that the board and chairman before Terence Brown were rubbish, too. There is a mindset in this club that makes us look like King Midas in reverse.

This is a club that refuse to sanction the purchase of a 34-year-old striker deemed 'too old' but who then give the go-ahead to buy him two years later.

This is a club that 'cashed in' on one of the best central defenders in Europe and still managed to lose £10m on the deal when the player moved again 18 months later. And let's not forget the 18-mill they did receive was wasted in a way that Viv Nicholson (ask yer Mum) would have viewed with envy. Let's not fool ourselves. Now matter how good the squad, how favourable the draw, how glowing the new dawn – West Ham will always find ways to **** up.

The problem is that the sickness eventually seeps into the fans' minds, too. A lot of people have written to me and suggested we sack Roeder and replace him with Micky Adams. 'Look how well he is doing for Leicester,' said one correspondent. Well, I'm sorry, but is that the best we can do? Someone who is doing well with the bankrupt Foxes? If that's the attitude we may as well stick with GR and see how well he does when/if we try and get out the First Division next year. This season might be the making of him. Or not. In any case, it makes no difference. Glenn Roeder was the easy option two seasons back and he's still the easy option now.

So is all this defeatist talk from the Blagger, I hear you cry? Well, yes it is actually. This column has never been about insightful tactics, insider gossip and tub-thumping vitriol. It's about constant anger, occasional joy, jaw-dropping bemusement and deep, dark depression. It's about being a fan of the most frustrating, annoying and underachieving football club ever to pull on 22 boots. And that means at times gloom and despondency sets in and nothing can shift it. This is such a week.

Next week I'll wave my red card and call for the head of Mr. Brown. Next week, I'll inquire if Mr. Roeder is the worst manager ever to tread the touchline since Mr. W.J. Blagg esq. gave up the reins at Mooros' one Sunday lunchtime. But this week my mood matches the place I'm in.

Good night from Birkenhead.

BLAGG, today

But, as all fans know, every season has its high and for the Hammers it arrived in February. On a televised 'live' match in the last week of the month, West Ham won a crucial game, 2-1, at West Brom and started an impressive run of results that ended with Glenn Roeder receiving the Manager of the Month award, which just went to show what a capricious beast football can be.

It would be nonsense to suggest that the Hammers could sense survival but a good gap had opened up between third from bottom West Ham and the two adrift below them. It was now up to the club to try and drag others into the melee – and that was what started to happen. Leeds and Bolton started glancing nervously over their shoulder as the Hammers picked up points. The season entered spring and there was everything to play for.

However, in an amazing three-day twist late in April, in a fashion so dramatic that it would be rejected as a storyline too far fetched for Sky's Dream Team, West Ham and Glenn Roeder were suddenly confronted with a whole different set of problems.

The Hammers' fans were about to witness another bizarre twist in what was fast becoming a fateful season.

Chapter 7

CARETAKER MANAGER
The legend returns

An almost inevitable late season rally gave West Ham hope of Premiership salvation as Glenn Roeder claimed the Barclaycard Manager of the Month award for March after guiding his side to two wins and a draw. The key game now was the away fixture against Bolton Wanderers.

In what football pundits call a six-pointer; West Ham faced Sam Allardyce's side with just a handful of games to go. Defeat was reckoned to be the Premiership death knell for either side.

And it was West Ham who lost the match, their tempers and, ultimately, their way as Wanderers' hero Jay-Jay Okocha scored a goal of quality to leave West Ham struggling. The match finished with Hammers' players fighting in the centre circle and losing their dignity along with the points.

Then, two days later, on Easter Monday, April 21, 2003, following a vital 1-0 win over Middlesbrough at Upton Park, came the shock news that Glenn Roeder had been rushed to hospital in a serious condition. Rumours of heart attack and blood clots – probably stress-related – were rife before it was revealed that Roeder had collapsed due to a brain tumour. Doctors said that this illness couldn't be caused by the stresses and strains of Premiership football and Roeder himself later confirmed this to be true. To this day many of us wonder, though, about the unknown links between illness and stress.

Dealing with the severe illness of someone who is being reviled in many quarters was one of the hardest things to report on. The fact that it was virtually impossible to find one single fan who thought that Roeder should have still been managing the side at the time of his illness, and that most of us would have done anything to be rid of his stewardship, was an irony lost on no-one.

Further complicating the matter was the inevitable question of 'would West Ham remain rudderless in a relegation dogfight'? And how could you ally this issue with a man possibly fighting for his very life? It was a difficult few weeks in the life of Online but, I'm proud to say, I thought the fans were magnificent in their support of Glenn Roeder, the man and West Ham fan, while, for the most part, sensitively handling the questions regarding the immediate future of the club.

BLAGG, Apr 2003

Football is never a simple matter, is it?

Like most of you, I suspect, I spent most of last Saturday night in a foul mood following, not just a decisive defeat in a game we had to win, but a performance that seemed totally lacking in anything resembling a modicum of tactical nous or creativity.

To see the Hammers undone by a flair player like Okocha – the type of player we might have expected to ply his trade at the 'Academy' in more enlightened times – was a deeply depressing sight. We are often outfought but rarely 'outskilled'. This time the fight was there but, sadly, it was reserved for punching any available referee, player or wall. We had two shots on target according to the papers but, if they were shown on TV, then I must have dozed off and missed them.

For anyone listening on the radio, Tony Gale's Capital Gold commentary summed things up admirably. So incensed was our old defender that he actually swore twice in the second half and I feared for his broadcasting future as he seemed fit to burst in the last 10 minutes. With the terminal expletives just a breath away, Gale was not slow in giving his opinion that the tactics and formation were totally wrong for this particular game and, sadly, it was difficult to disagree with him.

After a day of gloom and despondency, the preposterous

optimism of the average football fan was proved once again by an unsatisfying but deserved victory over a lack-lustre Middlesbrough. "Surely we can win all the remaining games?" we asked as our heads swam with the elation brought on by a home win and an overdose of chocolate eggs.

And then we heard about Glenn Roeder . . .

Now whatever you think of the man as West Ham manager, Glenn has always acted with dignity and decorum and, football being a game, I would never wish harm or bad health on anyone connected to the sport. Ironically, of course, the manager's health problems only go to prove that despite what many may think of his calm and unemotional exterior, inside Glenn was just as worried and frustrated as we all are.

As someone who listened to the Bolton game sitting alone in a car (it's not fair to drag others into your private hell) and staring intently at a couple of seagulls on a playing field, shaking with nerves and not able to drive for fear of harming other road users, it's easy to see how this ridiculous game shreds your nerves and raises your blood pressure. The pressure on a brave and honourable man must have been enormous. Too many accused Glenn Roeder of not caring but I think now we all know he cared a great deal.

Getting to the root of the problems with the club this season has been extremely difficult. I can, and have, criticised some of Glenn's decisions but I have always been quick to acknowledge the poor support that he has received from other quarters.

Certainly the players themselves have not been blameless. Have a look at our defensive record this season and view Tomas Repka's mindless shove on Villa's Allback last week. After weeks of criticism for not playing Fredi Kanouté for a full 90 minutes how did the Frenchman repay his manager last Saturday?

Read Harry Redknapp's 'amusing' tale of Paolo 'cut me and I bleed claret and blue' Di Canio's £10k pay rise after he refused to play against Spurs a couple of years back after a 'big club' (Chelsea) had offered him a contract and double wages.

And let's not forget the part paid by our illustrious

Chairman, a man who offers his old manager the price of a house in Chigwell not to spend any more money and then adds his moniker to a couple of multi-million pound cheques to purchase two players of dubious pedigree. A man who allows the sale of two players totalling nearly £30m and then pleads poverty when pestered for the price of a decent centre-half.

Make no mistake. Glenn Roeder may have made mistakes this season – and I'm not going to pretend that had I been West Ham chairman then Glenn Roeder would have been looking for a new job as early as last November (2002) – but he has been poorly aided by those who should know better. And when it comes down to it, didn't we want him to do well? GR is a local lad, the Hammers are his club and the claret and blue probably runs through his veins (no sick jokes please!) faster than an imported Italian with a dubious view of morality.

Hell, I might not have shouted this too loudly this season but I've prayed that Glenn could turn things around and come out of this with head held high. I've wanted him to do well more than any manager in my long years supporting the club.

By a bitter irony, lying in intensive care, Glenn Roeder is now earning the respect that he was probably due all along, at a time that he would probably have received it the least. I don't know if our manager will continue to occupy the Upton Park hot seat next season but it would be a small-minded person who didn't wish him a full and speedy recovery and hope that the club could pull off a minor miracle (aww – what the hell, a MAJOR miracle) and avoid the 'pleasures' of Nationwide League football.

Let's hope some of those others who helped put Glenn Roeder where he is today are taking a good look at themselves.

Tony the Driver
Get well soon, Glenn

Rhysm
Look, we all want Roeder to get well because he is a nice bloke. But I don't regret saying that he was a bad manager. I

didn't boo him Saturday but I have booed him before. It is a way of showing dissatisfaction. Don't get me wrong – if I was Glenn and got offered the West Ham job I would take it, too, but I think he is a terrible manager – not a terrible man. I think he is a good bloke who cares, but isn't a good enough manager. Get well soon.

Fred

All this sympathy for Roeder is well deserved, but only for his personal health. I can't stand the cynical prats who are now guilt-ridden for slagging him off for doing a crap job. The simple facts are he was doing a crap job and is not capable of managing WHU. He could have realised this earlier, when it was plain for all of us to see, and resigned. He decided against this in the deluded belief he could turn things around, which he could not. I don't blame Roeder totally for this and it is Brown, the chairman, who kept Roeder in a position way above his station simply because he was the cheap option. I hope Mr Brown is the one who is guilt-ridden, for it is he alone who allowed this situation to develop by not replacing Roeder and not recognising the levels of stress the poor guy was enduring.

Peatburn

I can't believe a man is in a coma, fighting for his life, and you're all arguing over whose fault it is. Brown, Di Canio, the fans, Repka and the players, it's absolutely nobody's fault what's happened to Glenn Roeder.

Upton Parker

I can't understand why there has been no statement from our captain about the situation.

KLM

Why should Di Canio respond to this situation in a way that meets your needs? I have not heard sympathetic comments to Glenn from about 30 players at the club, (Paul) Goddard, (Roger) Cross, the directors, the tea lady, etc, but I presume they are all concerned. Must they all make public statements to satisfy vigilantes?

Johnnie Boy

As club captain, PDC has a responsibility to the club, squad and fans to stand up and be counted. This is our hour of need. We need leaders and PDC has shown his true colours.

If you can't see that then you should open your eyes. We need shot of him, his petulance and lack of commitment.

And I am not a vigilante. I am a very angry fan.

Onliner

Paulo was vocal in his criticism of Glenn, and is now as vocal in his silence. You may be right, he doesn't need to respond to vigilantes, but a simple "get well soon, Glenn" would not hurt him. For me it demonstrates one thing: that PDC is no longer part of West Ham. It's time to say goodbye to the man and all his traits.

AdamL

Excellent piece, as ever. A lot of people are criticising Di Canio over his silence but now he's been quoted as saying this:

"Trying to blame players is nothing short of a disgrace; everyone at the club has to take responsibility for our results this season.

"I think the press have been on Glenn's back for the last six months and they are the ones who have created added pressure. The most important thing at the moment is that Glenn gets better as quickly as possible and I hope the team can do something special, to stay up for him.

"I made a conscious decision to remain quiet recently because everything I said was getting misrepresented, but I'd like now to take this opportunity to express my sadness at the present situation and to wish my manager the best of luck in his recovery from illness.

"We may have had our differences on the pitch but Glenn is a good man and my thoughts are with him and his family."

Sounds fair enough to me.

Johnnie Goat

Well said, Billy. With what happened with (Gerard) Houllier a while back, and Joe Kinnear and Jock Stein, you'd think

people would have learnt. I have not been happy this
season, but has Glenn hidden? No. Yes, he has made some
bad signings. But how else could he try and strengthen the
squad? No money or support from the board. It's been
scandalous that a team like Birmingham can sign four
players on transfer deadline day to keep them up and we
can't. The players have been shocking – Repka is a one-
man relegation waiting to happen. 'Sincs' has been jaded all
year. Fredi is woefully injury prone, then rubbish when he
gets a game.

When our most committed players are kids, help-the-aged
contenders, a goalkeeper and Steve Lomas, then we were
always going to suffer. Our players in the 24-33-year-old age
bracket have been awful and shown no interest.

But worst of all, our captain, playmaker and inspiration –
not Joey – PDC, well I idolised him. But this season, I have
never seen a player so single-mindedly undermine the
manager, club and squad so effectively.

My brother-in-law is Sheffield Weds and he always
maintained that PDC would be our undoing, like he was
theirs. The man makes me sick. No pride, no passion, no
loyalty, no guts, no strength, no decency, no love for the
club, nothing. Just a whingeing little man who's squandered
his talent and blames all and sundry instead of looking at
himself

GR is a good man – I wish him all the best. I'd rather he's
OK and we go down. Football's a game and though it'll
break my heart to be in the First Division, compared to a
good man's life, it means Sweet FA.

Either way, Glenn – get well soon

RDM

I sincerely hope he makes a full recovery and gets back to
his family. BUT, I don't want him as manager at my club any
longer. A lot of threads and feedback are blaming the
players this year – and yes, they have under-performed for a
lot of the season: James, Repka, Dailly, Breen, Schemmel,
Sinclair, Carrick, Kanouté (when he plays), PDC and now
Bowyer have all played really poorly. But it's the manager's
job to coach, guide and motivate them to play together. The
tactics, set pieces, and lack of imagination in selections of

the team have resulted in this mess and GR is the manager, so it IS his fault.

I'm sorry he's ill, but it is a fact that the problem lies at his doorstep, as he's sadly not good enough for a Premiership club.

Paolo

Blagg, you do talk some crap but this time you have hit the nail on the head. Well said, old boy.

Clack

Look, what's happened to Glenn Roeder is nobody's fault. It's scandalous to blame the players, the fans, Paolo Di Canio or even the chairman. By all means, let's discuss football but for people to start arguing over whose fault it is that a man has suffered a stroke, is just not on.

Baron von Evilswine

Like every manager, player and fan from clubs across the country, I wish Glenn a speedy recovery to full health.

However, I am not sure it is fair to blame the players or the fans for Roeder's stroke. When they wired Bolton boss Allardyce up during research on the stress of management, his heart rate went from 85 to 190 bpm during a game.

This is equivalent to the trauma of a car accident, only it happens to Allardyce (and presumably all other managers) once or twice a week. Is this the fans' fault, or the players?

To say that this stress is player or fan-induced is a gross simplification and ignores the internal pressures placed on managers by their own desire to succeed.

jack flash

An excellent article, BB, and here's to a speedy recovery for Glenn. This season has been the worst nightmare that I can remember in the last 40 years of supporting the Irons.

Worst, because although we've suffered relegation plenty of times before, this time we're going down with a squad of good, young talented players who will undoubtedly not hang around in the Nationwide and this time the stakes (-£20m Sky money) are far higher than ever before. I don't believe that our predicament rests entirely on Glenn's shoulders either – look what the same team of players achieved last season.

As you rightly (and obviously) point out, with the sale of £30m worth of talent there should have been enough in the kitty to buy a half-decent centre-half to accompany Repka – and therein lies the problem that has confounded the club for the last 40 years – the curse of the Cearns, if you like.

Mokum hammer

With a bit of luck, and a bit more support from the board and fans, he could have been THE man. But no-one could say he wasn't 100 per cent West Ham. For that reason, get well soon, Glenn

Dev

BB – I don't think we should talk about the performance of the club this season and the condition of Glenn Roeder in the same thread. To do so just seems to invite more criticism of him, which, in the present circumstances, is akin to kicking the man while he's down.

I'm also struggling with my own feelings of guilt right now. Those who have criticised Roeder in the past (like me), called him names or booed him, may be feeling uncomfortable about expressing their real opinions as to the reasons behind this disastrous season, partly as a result of feeling some (however small) degree of responsibility for what has happened to our manager.

Under these circumstances, it is hard, if not impossible, for anyone to make any reasoned judgements as to the reasons behind the poor performances and, even less, to equate them to the horrible events of the last 48 hours.

For example, in this article, you just end up blaming other people (players, board, Redknapp), which probably goes against what you may have said in the past, or at least spreads the blame more widely than it might have done a few days ago?

No right-minded fan would EVER have wanted to see this happen to Glenn Roeder. He is undoubtedly a very committed man who has tried as hard as he possibly can to deliver results for West Ham United. For that, and that alone, he deserves our full support in this, his greatest hour of need. Right now, everything else is secondary.

Sutton soul hammer
Nice one, Bill - keep the faith, you never know... :-)

Regarding Brown, here's a man who's putting too much pressure on a manager ill-equipped to compete at this level, then providing no funds at the start of the season, while previously mis-managing the club into such a position that we failed to attract any decent candidates in the first place.

Good luck to Glenn, you're right, I think most of us would love to see him triumph, but even you side with Galey's opinion that, tactically, we've been far too naivé this season. When are we gonna be a professionally run club? If we go down, it may be too late to ever rebuild. Gutted.

Davey B
I sincerely hope that Glenn recovers soon. I, like many others, couldn't understand why he didn't rant and rave on the touchline and show the same emotions that I did. I was so clearly wrong in ever doubting this man's devotion to our cause. For thinking that thought, I feel so guilty and I am truly sorry to have ever doubted you, Glenn.

It would be justice if he recovers and goes on to become a great manager of our famous club so that he can throw it back in the face of those disgraceful so-called supporters who verbally abused him.

A friend of mine was witness to these mindless idiots who purport to support our club on Saturday and had the guts to confront them, but is now being advised by the club to avoid that particular part of the ground in the future for his trouble.

Tony M
Good article, Blagg. I agree with pretty much all you say and it's just a shame it takes something like this for a lot of people to realise that Glenn Roeder does care for West Ham.

Blunders
I finally realised last Friday that there are more important things than the beautiful game, especially people's health.

My girlfriend was rushed into hospital on Friday after she'd collapsed and I've been worried and stressed out ever since. The relegation struggle of the last week has gone completely over my head and I even went to Bolton! That day was just a blur.

I've had no time to get upset or worry about West Ham and, really, it's made me accept our relegation lightly. After all (I never thought I'd ever hear myself say this) it IS only a game.

Paulo Di Godlo

Totally agree, let's all wish him a quick recovery – but I have to disagree on one thing. "I think now we all know he cared a great deal". What a load of crap! My grandfather had a stroke when he was under 50 and then a heart attack after he'd retired. I don't think it's 'cos he cared about West Ham but rather because sometimes people get ill. To say that Roeder is ill, therefore this proves anything at all, is nonsense. Of course he cares, of course he always has done. I know that deep down – not because he's ill but because I do!

BLAGG, today

With Glenn Roeder in hospital and real fears for his health, it took a big man to undertake the chance to lead the Hammers from the clutches of relegation. Step forward, West Ham United and England legend Trevor Brooking.

No sooner was Brooking announced as caretaker manager 'until further notice' than the team suddenly showed what could have been achievable earlier in the season, embarking on a run of wins and draws that, on the form at the time, was equalled only by the top two sides in the Premiership. At least that was how it seemed.

In actual fact, the team had put a good run together under Roeder and there had been a vast improvement in the team's fortunes since the win over West Brom at The Hawthorns a month earlier but, unfortunately, the crucial loss at Bolton blighted that run.

Under Brooking, important points were accrued at Manchester City although a draw at home to Aston Villa, a side who hadn't won away all season was, in some ways,

just as costly as the Bolton defeat. Eventually, though, only
two games remained: one at home to Chelsea and the other
away to Birmingham City and, even though there was still a
possibility that the situation may be out of their own hands,
at least the Hammers were in with a fighting chance

BLAGG, May 2003

Well, if nothing else it's getting bloody exciting, isn't it?
And, foolish though it may seem, I've even started to believe
the impossible may just be within reach.

My optimism is built on the idea that, despite putting a
fantastic run together in the last nine games or so, the
Hammers haven't really shown fully what they are capable
of. Our wins have often been scrappy, nervous and
unconvincing. In the circumstances I'll accept that, of
course, but I'd just like to see a bit of the old Hammers
swagger return.

So I have this feeling we're due a big performance with an
impressive win – and what better way for it to arrive than
against the Champions League-chasing (is there a bigger
oxymoron in sport?) Chelsea?

If, and it's still a big IF, we get three points against the
Blues then surely anything is possible in the last game? I'd
make some comments about heart pills, etc, but, sadly, they
may appear a little tasteless given recent events.

Still, this is a good time to turn the Blagger spotlight onto
our new wonderful caretaker manager. Please take a bow,
Sir Trevor Brooking! Anyone lucky enough to see this great
footballer in action will purr with pleasure at the many
memories this one-club man gave the claret and blue
faithful.

On a personal level, if I could return a fully fit former player
to our ranks today, then Trev would be up there just behind
the inevitable Mooro. The number of games I saw 'Geno'
win almost single-handedly are almost too many to recount
and I just sit here with a silly grin on my fat face as I
remember some sublime performances in our Division Two
title season of 1980-81 as Trevor worked on a different plane
against players who just seem honoured to share the same
pitch space. If you ever see me down the pub, buy me a
pint and I'll regale you of a performance against Shrewsbury

that still gives goosebumps to this day.

Sadly, as is the way of the world, Trevor's move into football punditry saw him recast as a rather amusing, often bumbling, middle-aged man probably best portrayed in Alistair McGowan's hilarious impression. Nowhere did this fall from grace strike more fiercely than round at Blagg Acres. For it was here, one fine summer day in 1988, that No.1 son, Blagg Jnr, was named after the aforementioned Mr Brooking. "Why did you name me after someone who wears a C&A suit on *Match of the Day*?' the little scamp frequently used to ask me as soon as he was big enough to talk.

Of course it wasn't always like that. Back when little lad was a baby, I had the opportunity of attending a book signing where Trevor was adding his dabs to anyone kind enough to fork out £15 for the tome, *101 Great Footballers*.

As I was ushered into Trevor's sanctum he asked me what I wanted him to sign in the book.

"It's for my son – he's only nine-months-old and he's named after you," I stammered. Trevor found this greatly amusing and not a little touching.

"I'm honoured," he replied, "So do you want me to put anything else other than 'To Trevor'?"

"But he's name's not Trevor," I pointed out.

The Maestro looked a little puzzled at this.

"But I thought you said . . ."

"Yeah, sorry, I'm confusing you. His name is Brooking, not Trevor. I mean, no disrespect, but Trevor is an 'orrible name."

For some reason everyone found this to be particularly amusing and the book signing degenerated into fits of giggles and suppressed coughing. I could never see what was so funny myself.

Anyway, one of the more pleasurable moments this season has been to ring my son up and inform him with pride that the real Mr Brooking was back and, once more, he could swan around the classroom taunting his enemies and puffing his chest out. If Trevor brings us three victories then I think Blagg Jnr may well be the toast of the playground once again. This will be particularly pleasing as a certain Mr Curbishley has a son in the same class.

Welcome back to the real world, Trevor – and let's hope Alistair McGowan's next impression is of a man with arms aloft celebrating the start of a new religion.

D.Rollo

Ladies, Gentleman and miscellaneous others, I give you Trevor Brooking. Please forgive me if this descends into overly emotional gayness. Please understand if, driven as I am by the aforementioned emotion, this turns out to be bollocks of the highest order.

How much do we owe this man? Board stooge? Well, perhaps. Genuine, copper-bottomed 100 per cent confirmed West Ham legend? Hell, yeah! OK, he had that title before his foray into the world of diagrams on blackboards and touchline posturing, but it stands truer than ever now.

Some things just go together: Toast and Marmite, Barbarella and thigh length boots; Brooking and West Ham. It's about dignity and pride. The fans never lost it but the club had. Brooking restored it, almost instantly.

The Roeder regime is a shambles. It always felt like something could go wrong. Even with things going well he never seemed like the man for it. Whatever his positives (and yes, there are some), it just didn't feel right.

But when you see Brooking standing there, resplendent in whichever shade of brown suit he's chosen, loving being involved, loving helping his club, just loving his club, it really does feel right. In a lot of ways Brooking is a throwback to a forgotten football time, a decent man who gives credit where it's due but isn't afraid to admit to his and the players' mistakes. Brooking has integrity. Brooking doesn't flinch.

Trevor Brooking, a hero of West Ham's past, has helped rescue the present and the future, given the young 'uns an idea of his stature at the club, his love for the club. A true gent, a decent bloke, a real man, a Hammer and a 100 per cent West Ham legend.

brownout

How depressingly West Ham. A manager horribly out of his depth finally removed in just about the worst way imaginable. Replaced by our favourite son, bringing a brief flicker of hope but all the while that nagging feeling that he just doesn't have enough time.

NorthBanker
You just know we're going to beat Chelsea now, don't you? God, I love that man!

BLAGG, today
In one of the best matches seen at Upton Park in recent times, roared on by a capacity crowd West Ham scored a fantastic 1-0 victory at Upton Park over Champions League-bound Chelsea. Old Boy Frank Jnr returned to torment us, and very nearly scored, but substitute Paolo Di Canio got the goal in what was confidently expected – rightly in this case – to be his last home game for the club. The Italian's celebrations were matched only by that of the crowd. Was the greatest escape since Steve McQueen last threw a baseball against a concrete wall still on?

Unfortunately, in one of those horrible incidents that seem to dog West Ham United, Sky had decided to select the Southampton v Bolton game as their live match on Saturday evening. Consequently, knowing the result from Upton Park, Bolton, the only side the Hammers could catch in their relegation fight, decided to shut up shop at St. Mary's stadium and managed to thwart the Saints in a 0-0 bore draw.

This meant the Hammers' fate was out of their own hands. On the final day of the season, Bolton faced a home game to Middlesbrough, needing only a draw to confirm their safety, while West Ham headed for St Andrews to meet Birmingham City, knowing that even a win there might not be enough if Bolton did all they had to do at the Reebok.

Chapter 8

RELEGATION IS SUCH AN
UGLY WORD

Despite the splendid efforts of Sir Trevor, West Ham's attempt to stay up faltered at the last hurdle. Bolton's home win against a Middlesbrough side barely going through the motions looked to be the final kick in the teeth until we realised that the eventual 2-2 draw the Hammers gained at St. Andrew's actually meant that the side finished with 42 points – the highest total ever obtained by a side going down and a total that would have virtually granted us mid-table status the following season.

Even more staggering was the fact that the Hammers had lost 15 games in the 2002-03 season when they finished seventh and yet they lost only one more game the following campaign yet had been relegated. Even at our lowest ebb there was a touch of bad luck against us.

I'd seen relegation before and it's always horrible. But this time there was much more to lose. There was unlikely to be the commitment made to the club by players as there was in 1978, when West Ham were able to parade a second division side almost the same as the one that was relegated. In the late 80s and early 90s yo-yo years the players were of such poor quality that relegation had made little difference.

Now, though, there was a real concern about what state West Ham would start the following season.

Within 24 hours of the finality of relegation from the Premiership, young star striker Jermain Defoe had handed in a transfer request in sickening fashion. Brooking described his request as 'misguided' and assured fans that no decisions had yet been made on what would happen to players, although some would 'obviously' be moving on. Shortly after, Terence Brown announced there would be no 'fire sale'.

But for most of the fans the realisation of relegation had hardly had time to sink in...

BLAGG, May 2003

Relegation is such an ugly word, isn't it? It has a harsh, distressing quality to it and you almost have to contort your face to get the unruly syllables out of your mouth. It's not nice to say and it's definitely not nice to experience.

Let me start by saying I am very, very upset and very, very angry. I'm not sure if I'm more one than the other, and the prime emotion changes with my mood, but I do know that I'm finding this relegation pretty difficult to stomach.

Now this is not going to be one of those 'Life/Death/Football' rants. I know what's important in life. I knew that whatever transpired at St. Andrew's and the Reebok on Sunday, I was going to spend part of Monday at an aunt's funeral with a large West Ham-supporting family contingent, and the atmosphere was going to be pretty grim whatever happened.

But supporting West Ham is important to many of us and I know there were an awful lot of tears in an awful lot of eyes on Sunday. The prospect of facing up to Wimbledon next season is something that has upset a great number of honest, hard-working people who invest a lot of time, love, money and effort into this club of ours.

Blagg Jnr didn't say too much on Sunday. He's quite stoical about his football and, left to his own devices, he probably won't be an Upton Park regular like his father. Nevertheless, I could see in his eyes that he was upset – and that made me feel worse. I want to get hold of these players, the management and coaching staff – but particularly the board – and ask them how in God's name they managed to get us into this mess. Just look at those players, look at the money they receive, look at the set-up at this club of ours, the stadium, the history.

Relegation in the 2002-03 season is a disgrace to the

community that West Ham represents and a nadir in our history.

Now before you all write in, I'm a lot of things but I'm not stupid. I know that some of those who kiss the badge were born in far-flung fields and they have no real feel for the club, its supporters and its heritage. I also know football has changed and the attitude of the sporting superstars who play the game today differs greatly from the days when we could sign a striker from Newcastle United and expect him to provide us with total and utter commitment.

But, paradoxically of course, of all the clubs where relegation could have occurred, how ironic that it happens at a place where bringing young, home-grown talent through has been the rule rather than the exception. Many of our players are local lads; our manager is an East End boy. Of all the places where the staff might be expected to feel as bad as the supporters, Upton Park is a prime location.

Lack of investment over the close season – particularly in providing a fourth striker and a decent centre-half – got us off to a bad start. The failure to produce a top quality defender in the transfer window was an appalling error of judgement although the introduction of seasoned professionals Les Ferdinand and Rufus Brevett at the same point showed just what had been missing previously in terms of top class professionalism. I feel sorry for both of them.

Sadly, it has to be said that any other club in the country would have replaced their manager after the home defeat by Leeds United or, at the latest, the embarrassment at Villa Park in November and Glenn Roeder has to bear the brunt of a lot of the criticism for this season's failure. What galled me most, though, was the lack of application, passion and plain old common sense that characterised defeats and draws at the hands of West Bromwich Albion, Birmingham City, Southampton, Fulham and Bolton Wanderers. And when you have to play your best defender (Ian Pearce) as a centre-forward for a month, then it's time to blow your whistle, stop and have a bloody good look at what is happening.

Other reasons? Kanouté's groin strain seemed to last for nine months and makes me wonder what the hell Fredi has dangling between his legs to provide him with such problems. On a personal level, I believe a forward should get you 15+ goals a season, minimum, and I've always been ambivalent towards the Frenchman for this reason. Offers above £6m should be immediately accepted.

Bowyer was a good gamble that never came off due to injury. Breen also seemed a worthwhile punt (no pun intended) but he was to suffer post-traumatic World Cup syndrome – the same affliction that cruelly struck down Trevor Sinclair – and ended up being a disgraceful joke.

And talking of jokes, have you heard the one about the Hammer of the Year who didn't bother turning up for the following season? Sebastian Schemmel, a man who has now opened a chip shop in Southend with Elvis and Martin Boorman. Appalling.

Cole struggled manfully and was our best player without ever seeming to unlock defences in the way that we all hoped. Carrick was fitful at best but was also cruelly struck with a mysterious injury that seems to keep only West Ham players out of contention for such long periods. Di Canio was . . . well, Di Canio actually! And it just made you curse that footballing syndrome, often know as the 'Best Gascoigne Bowles Dilemma', that maintains that to be a genius with the ball means you have to carry an enormous amount of mental baggage to offset it.

James provided both proof of why he is expected to take over David Seaman's gloves for England while also showing why the pony-tailed one hasn't been put under pressure despite approaching his 40th birthday. I do think James has provided the appropriate amount of contrition for his part in the relegation saga and I was impressed by his willingness to offer to stay next season and try to atone for the number of goals he has conceded in this. However, I think we can get good money for DJ and a quality replacement for a fraction of the price.

Nevertheless, taking everything into account, there is no way this squad of players should have been relegated this season. They are undoubtedly the most gifted bunch ever to set foot in the Nationwide and all of them – including management, board and coaching staff – should hang their heads in shame. Please don't write and tell me I'm being harsh on someone or other – I don't care.

On a personal level, I have been struggling to pay the mortgage and keep mind and soul together since last May and West Ham's season had coincided with my own Annus Horribilus. Just one week's wages from any of these prima donnas would solve my problems and if any of them want to swap my place in the sun for theirs, then bring it on!

Finally, though, a word about Jermain Defoe. Unfortunately that word is unprintable. What disgusting, gutless and pitiful excuse can you possible make for handing in a transfer request the morning after you have been relegated? I fully expect to hear next that the only reason the request wasn't received on the same afternoon was the ref's pencil broke as they came off the pitch.

The lad's only defence is just that – he is a lad. In which case, if I see him in that Romford restaurant that Lady B frequents again, he can expect a clip round the ear and sent to his bedroom for a week. Jermain, my boy – you're NOT 'Pop' Robson. Not by a long f******** way. You may be only 20 but you're not even Michael Owen.

You were ever-present this season and played well but 11 goals is a poor return even with the service you received. Did you not contribute to the failure this year, then? Did you think your misses against Aston Villa a few weeks back still counted in some way? You're still young and you may be ambitious and hungry. You may want success. But you also need pride and humility. You need to stand up and be counted, not scuttle off because things didn't go your own way when you stamped your foot.

Success may be better served with a Division One title to tuck in that very large hat you seem intent on buying.

Whatever happens, your poor timing and ill conceived, self-serving remarks (commendation to Tony Gale for his 'before the fans tears have dried' speech) rank among the lowest contributions to a profession long known for the paucity of its intelligence and honour.

Am I missing something here? Wasn't this Defoe's first season as a fully-fledged first team member? Surely only Kanouté's long-term injuries stopped him being confined to bench-warming for periods. Absolutely astonishing! I would hold this snivelling kid to at least another year of his two-term contract and trust he learns some lessons in that time. And then, when he goes – and he most certainly will – let's make sure we get sell-on contracts to enable us to earn £15m+ off the back off this wonder boy (no more Rio carve-ups please!). Perhaps then we can wish him luck as he cavorts off to Real Madrid or somewhere else where his undoubted skill and massive ego will be truly appreciated. Doubt it, though.

Do you know the truly galling thing here, though? While I've been writing this I have received a phone call from Lady Blagg. Sinclair, Carrick and Minto have dropped into the shop where the missus is working and have spent half-an-hour admiring the goods (and I don't mean on the shelves!) before giving her a kiss and disappearing next door for a long lunch and a relaxing afternoon.

A response to the Good Lady's "commiserations on relegation"?

"Ah well, it happens!"

What? It happens? Yeah, at Upton Park it always f******** happens. You see there are a lot of people to blame for relegation this season. There are a lot of people suffering. But they are not necessarily one and the same. The only ones who are truly blameless in this – the only ones who care enough – are the very ones who suffer the most. That's the fans. You and me, matey. You and me.

The 2003-04 season – unless we win a Cup or get to a final, as in 1980-81 – will represent a waste of time in football terms. At best we'll walk away with the title and get back where we belong. At worst, we will struggle and face possible oblivion.

If we win promotion at the first time of asking, then the 2004-05 season will then become one of consolidation as we seek to replace makeshift players, who we patched in to help us gain promotion. Without a massive injection of something we currently lack it may be the end of the decade before we get back to where we were last summer.

Before this season my head has been away with the stars dreaming of Europe. Now, I'm looking at Crystal Palace and Millwall for my excitement. We had a generation of the finest young players ever to come from this (or any) club. What a waste. I'm seriously starting to despair of ever being 'young' enough to be able to celebrate anything of note ever again (promotions back to places you shouldn't have left in the first place don't count). I watch the loss of my hair, libido and football team and wonder if I ever believed it could have been different.

So what's next and where do we go from here? Well, that's obviously going to have to be discussed over the coming weeks and months. Is it too much to hope that just for once this club pulls itself up by its expensively laced boots and actually gives something back to the fans? Get shot of the deadwood (saving £10m on wages, according to this morning's paper) but keep everyone else – apart from those we chose to sell?

Get a couple of youngsters through to make us feel better about ourselves? Sell a holiday home or two and take a chance on someone like Bobby Zamora who may not be proven at the top level but will definitely provide something we'll need next season?

And what about putting something into place that assures us of a longer run in the Premiership when – please not if - we get back next season? I'm not asking for Arsenal or Manure – but surely we can be as 'big' as Southampton?

'Bubbles' has been the West Ham anthem since the 1920s. Consider the words 'Fortunes always hiding' and 'then like my dreams they fade and die'. Do you really think that is a coincidence? West Ham United FC has underachieved throughout its history and, whatever happens, unless this club addresses the very basic issue of how it perceives itself then Blagg Jnr may well find himself comforting his own tearful offspring some 40 years hence.

If only those employed by the club could match the pride, passion, commitment and love of those who support it.

This has been a sad, sad week.

Gutted-hammer
Relegation? Noooooooooooooooooooooooooo...

Fred
You make sense in a great deal of what you say, Blagg, but the one thing that I wouldn't agree with is the point that the

fans are blameless. We knew what was happening. We've dreaded this from the moment Rodent was employed as manager. We've watched with increasing disbelief as the season unfolded, the terrible state of team affairs, created wholly by the manager and board, and we did nothing.

Pathetic attempts were made to make Brown aware of our outrage. Booing Rodent was the very minimum required. But in the main we sat and watched the demise of a potentially great team.

I have been a fan of PDC, the player, but not the person, but it took me a while to realise why he was spouting off in the press. He knew things were wrong, he knew Rodent wasn't up to the job. But I, like many, assumed he was a hot-head having a go for the sake of it.

I have let West Ham, the club, down by not reacting sooner and more effectively – we, the supporters, could and should have done a great deal more. Sure, the manager, chairman and players under-performed but in it's time of need we, who have a great deal of say after all, let it happen.

Martin Peters

Part of the attraction of supporting West Ham is that over the years, as a club, it has emphasised (not always successfully) the importance of loyalty (both in terms of managers and players). It still has (to a lesser extent) that small club feel about it. Brooking is the outstanding example - sticking with the club when it was relegated and he was a leading England international. That is so rare now and that is why Defoe's comments, and the point at which he made them, were so lacking in class.

Glen Johnson – you are now carrying the flag. I am becoming a big fan. I'm hoping Joey and Michael C will do likewise. Of course, there is a limit to everything, which is why the board's decision to still stick by Roeder is, in my view, misguided.

Dutch Courage

I'm afraid the official site is saying Roeder is here to stay. God help us now.

Strong Dreams

Today is the first day I have managed to bring myself to read anything about West Ham. I've been in denial. An excellent piece that I agree with 100 per cent. One observation that proves (to me at least) that there is good in the world is Glen Johnson's comments. He is totally committed to the club. I have always admired people for their loyalty and it's nice to see this type of loyalty in one so young and talented.

Roeder won't be back. The job is too stressful for somebody in his condition. Iain Dowie may be an option.

Krap not Pu

BB – THANK YOU, you have managed to put into words exactly what we all feel – the hurt is something I am having real problems coming to terms with. As you quite rightly stress, we now will have to endure a minimum of two seasons in the wilderness as we strive to get back to where we were. I, too, truly believe we have the potential to be the biggest club side in London but we will need to have men of vision at the helm, not the penny-pinching bunch we still have at present. I shall be at next week's bondholders' meeting and promise to be pretty vocal.

philofacts

BB – you may still feel crap, but somehow you have helped me and I now feel halfway normal for the first time since about 10-past three on Sunday.

RIP

Billy, mate. You are the true poet of the people. Poetic champions compose. Dweller on the threshold. Beautiful vision. As someone else so bootifully put in on another thread, better to have loved and lost than never to have loved.

Manse

Mr B, that goes down as the best piece I've ever read on this site, absolutely spot-on. But I wish you had not had to write it and me had to read it.

We, as fans, invest so much emotionally in this club and

are so appallingly served in return. I thought that the Worthington Cup 'Mannygate' mistake a few years ago hurt, but this is something else. I'm sure it didn't feel like this last time we went down. In fact, I know it didn't.

How can we MAKE them appoint a proper manager for next season? Somehow we've got to get through to the board.

Nemesis

Says exactly what I feel. I was ready for relegation weeks ago, or so I thought, but the reality of it is so ******* depressing. I feel so bloody angry about the waste of it all and the impotence of us fans. All we can do to protest is to stop going to games, and how does that help the club rebuild?

West Ham Utd FC do not deserve us.

Tacchini kid

Is there any way to get this piece to the club? Surely there has to be a way of getting someone to get this piece to the club and make those ******* see what they have done?

Thirsty

Excellent article, BB. The thing that unites us all is that we all share the same grief and the same anger.

Relegation is unacceptable, bearing in mind the talent and resources at the club and the options which were available.

It's the sheer bloody mindedness of the board which, as well as our inability to properly make them accountable for their actions, is so frustrating.

Our only strength, if we exercise it collectively, is not to renew our season tickets before the renewal date. As the respected voice, perhaps you should give a lead in this regard.

Midfield General

For three days I have managed to hold it in, not show too much anger and frustration, much to the surprise and disappointment of my friends who would love to rub it in more than I allow. But now, sat embarrassed at my desk at work (in front of a Wigan fan of all things), Blagg, I salute you for being only the third thing – behind Leon (that hit man and little Herr Flick) and a selection of women that have blighted my life – to bring a tear to my eye since I embarked on my journey into adulthood. A truly outstanding piece. Blagg for *The Sun*!

Beaklington

Outstanding contribution, Blagg. I totally agree with your sentiments.

Mansfield

Billy, agreed. The pivotal point in the season really was the home game against Leeds. At half time, at 3-0 down, Roeder's position was untenable. The 'spirited' second half display not only saved his skin but also ultimately condemned us to the Nationwide. I suspect next season will be a lot more difficult than a lot of us imagine.

chang klan

Serves you right for ever supporting our bunch of shite in the first place, Billy boy. But there again, like me, you probably had little choice in the matter. But would we want to support anyone else anyway? Basically we're just a bunch of mugs, no more than gate fodder for those whose pockets are so handsomely lined at our emotional and financial expense. Do the majority of those over-paid prima donnas who wear our shirt really give over 30 per cent commitment over the season (the obvious few exceptions noted)? Nevertheless an inspired rant, Mr Blagg. Anger always seems to induce the most articulate of passionate clarity among those who are so able.

Sandgroperhammer

Great article. The responsibility for this debacle falls squarely on our board. They appointed a decent human being as manager who was not up to the job. When all the signs were there to see, they did nothing, and in January failed to provide the funds needed to ensure safety. Compare our situation to that of Birmingham City.

Remember Mr Brown's comments in the Annual Report about supporters chasing "unprecedented success". Well, he got his way. We simply reverted to past form. Those who don't learn from past mistakes are bound to repeat them. Let's all ensure that these incompetents don't get a chance to repeat them again.

Could someone print out Blagg's comments and nail them to the front door of the club, so the appropriate people could read them. I'm sick of their under-performing.

Ozziehammer

Great read that sums up our collective thoughts, Billy. There is no doubt that relegation this year is a different kettle of fish from the past three that I have witnessed, because of the financial ramifications. But above anything else, whoever manages, what players we have left, what financial shit we are in, please, please, please let us NOT play the long ball tactic all ********* season. IT IS WITHOUT DOUBT THE SINGLE BIGGEST REASON FOR OUR RELEGATION THIS YEAR. It has been a revelation in the last few games to see James roll the ball out to defenders and how much better a side have we looked?

I swear that if Roeder is still there next year and I see James (no, hang on, I won't see West Ham at all next year, they won't be on Foxtel (Aussie network) – thanks) and I hear that James is playing the boot down the middle, I will come over there and . . . no, settle down Geoff, remember your blood pressure.

Boxa

Awesome piece, BB, can only agree and add nothing.

Lady Hammer

I never knew you could use such explicit language . . . bejesus!

But, as always, you are on the bloody ball, especially about Defoe. I could hardly believe my ears. What 'effing sauce, eh? Now, in my day . . .

clack

We've got in a mess 'cos having a good youth policy doesn't work anymore. All you're doing is feeding

Champions League teams with quality players. It's the wrong policy.

Deportivo La Coruna, a smaller club than WHU, cottoned on to that 10 years ago, virtually scrapped their youth system and spent the money on a world-wide scouting network instead, bringing in cheap but good talent. That policy has brought untold success, including the Spanish championship and regular Champions League qualification.

It shouldn't be like this but it is. Values like loyalty and producing home-grown players mean absolutely nothing in football nowadays, unless you're someone like Man U or Real Madrid who can afford a youth academy without fear of losing their best, young players.

Bolton got it right. It's a world market now and so many good international players are available cheap, or on loan, but we chose to give enormous salaries and contracts to average players like Cole, Carrick, Sinclair, etc, just 'cos they're English or home-grown. The old ways don't work anymore and WHU have learnt that the hard way and at some considerable expense.

I can't agree with the comment that this is one of the most talented squads to get relegated. One of the most over-hyped, yes.

Bill, Sydney, Oz

Brilliant summation of the season, Blagg.

I don't think you've left anything out, except possibly the 'supporters' who booed Glenn at the Middlesbrough game and the one who threw the bottle through his window. For me, those two incidents left a more bitter taste than even relegation did.

StR

If each and any of them had an ounce of honour or integrity they would resign right now, after being responsible for one of the biggest fiascos and ****-ups ever to befall a top flight football club. The fact that they all seem firmly fixed in place says it all.

JayeMPee

Good piece, BB, but the post that the board are keeping faith with Roeder is sickening.

I fail to understand how a management team (if that's what you call it) that has screwed up so badly can remain. We know there is no management integrity at UP. Well, clearly there is no honour or sense of responsibility either.

If this lot remain in post then, firstly, I don't understand what Brown meant when he apologised for mistakes which he maintained would be put right. And secondly, we can forget all prospects of going straight back up. Roeder will take us along the path of Sheffield Weds and QPR – he is not up to the job.

Casual Observer

I think you were a bit harsh on Defoe, being of the opinion that his agents have royally f****d up. You can't really blame him for wanting to go, can you?

Nels

Phew, how many words was that?

That's like all your insides building up all the season and you've just burst and let it all out. Can't fault it, though. It's what we all feel. We even had a chance to alter things in the transfer window – we needed a defender and a goalscorer and we bought a midfielder, Bowyer. The difference a few more thousand spent then, might have made now. A drop in the ocean compared to the millions we'll lose now. I wish we knew if any players actually bothered to visit this or any of the sites to see what the general view was of the people who pay their wages.

jack flash

Not much consolation but as the psychiatrist says to the manic-depressive: "Where do you see yourself 10 years from now?"

Like I said, not much consolation – but having supported West Ham for nearly 40 years, I would say: "About where we were about 10 years ago."

alfie romeo

Well written – and it's always something that has bugged me. A lot of West Ham fans are happy to accept that the club will never achieve anything. With arguably the greatest ever crop of youngsters in the team, we went down.

StR

Let's face it, any club with Brown, (Paul) Aldridge and Roeder in the three key jobs is a joke. The fact that it happens to be our club does not change that fact. What possible optimism can there be that these three hopeless cases can get us back up at the first time of asking? And even if they did, it would have to be a fluke, which could not last – like last season's seventh place.

Let's face it, with these three in charge we are well and truly f****d. And the thing is, they feed off each other – each of them knows that they are fairly safe whilst the other two are there.

Miss G

Great article, Blagg, you speak for many of us.

DJ.Oscar

Great article, shame it ever had to be written but a great read.

Mick the most

Blindin' piece – but I didn't think it would hurt this bad. F*** it hurts.

ironphilly

Three or four times a year I get on a plane and fly 7,000 miles to watch West Ham. I change schedule so that I don't miss them when they are on TV here in the States. I must say that my feelings are expressed perfectly there – thank you, Blagg, old boy. If you should ever find yourself in Philadelphia, all consumables will be on me!

Meanwhile, if they really are going to retain Roeder, I despair. Honourable, decent man he undoubtedly is, a football manager he most certainly isn't qualified to be.

Rhyme

Paul Aldridge has just been on the radio. He has said that he will stick with the team and with Glenn Roeder. I wish

Glenn well but this is another bit of crap that the board has put in to place.

BLAGG, today

Rumours were rife on just what exactly West Ham had to do now they faced at least a season out of the Premiership. The loss of the guaranteed Sky money meant that corners needed to be cut and players' salaries needed to be slashed. Nobody was in any doubt that things were about to change.

First off, though, was the heartening fact that many players were coming to the end of their contracts. Paolo Di Canio had already been told that his contract would not be renewed and elsewhere loan deals and barely missed fringe players were being released.

The loss of Di Canio was obviously viewed as significant but serious questions had been asked about his attitude in several key games throughout the previous season and it was thought that perhaps the time was right for a parting of the ways regardless of how the season panned out.

With sums of £10m being touted as the amount being saved by the club, hopes were high that things might be salvaged. Perhaps the loss of one or two top players wouldn't be such a bad thing – after all, it had to be remembered that most of these players had been so inept during the season that they had caused the crisis in the first place. Lacklustre Trevor Sinclair and misfiring Fredi Kanouté could surely be sacrificed?

Then came the shock news that the club had accepted a £6m offer from Chelsea for young full-back Glen Johnson. No-one outside of the club can perhaps understand the seismic reaction this had among fans.

At the time this looked a terrible decision and even hindsight has not softened the blow. Johnson had been introduced late in the season by Glenn Roeder in an attempt to plug the problem right-back position (indeed, his debut against Blackburn Rovers coincided with our first home win of the season). It was seen as a gamble at the time. Johnson was highly rated but plunging such a young player into a relegation dogfight could well have killed his fragile confidence and put his progress back years.

In fact, Glen was a revelation and many fans think that the

Hammers' late season fight back was due to the form of Johnson and the arrival of Rufus Brevett, as Nigel Winterburn's replacement on the left. Ironically, the under-fire manager had then actually been criticised for not bringing Johnson into the team earlier – slow-development had long been a criticism levelled at Harry Redknapp – but Glen Johnson may well have had a higher rating of Roeder's coaching ability as he joined Chelsea's growing army of superstars purchased from the millions of roubles now available from new owner Roman Abramovich.

It was not unreasonably assumed by the fans that, as a player with barely a handful of games under his belt, Johnson would form the new guard able to find their feet in the First Division. Joe Cole, Trevor Sinclair and David James would all surely attract bids – but Glen Johnson? If the selling of Rio Ferdinand said 'We are a selling club if the offer is right', then the sale of Glen said: 'Don't panic everyone! Don't panic' in a deranged Corporal Jones-type voice. It was the thin edge of a large wedge.

Before the new fixture lists had been printed West Ham had offloaded a team of current or future England internationals. The only two of the expected want-away players to stay were, bizarrely, James – now a certain starter for England – and the much-maligned Defoe, the one player who actually asked for a transfer.

Even the sums involved in the transfers were disappointing to the supporters. If anything was to soften the loss of Johnson – and not much could - £6m for a player with such a minimum amount of experience could be seen as good business (providing you have your eyes closed, of course).

However, even that financial crutch was to be kicked under us as, just before the new season was about to begin, Cole joined Johnson at Chelsea for a reported £6.5m. Rumours were that Sir Alex Ferguson had been preparing bids in excess of £15m just a year before and now the loss of West Ham's great white hope for the future had been stolen from us for barely a song.

Put in perspective, this meant that Cole had left for a little over a £1m more than West Ham had paid to secure the services of Don Hutchison from Sunderland barely a year previously. In a staggering piece of ill fortune, West Ham's *relegation from the top flight had coincided with the long-awaited transfer crash. The fact that this fall in transfer values had been the very thing that allegedly prompted the Rio sale a few seasons back, was an irony lost on few.*

As the new season approached West Ham could only glance enviously over to Stamford Bridge where Johnson and Cole had joined Lampard in the Blues' first team. It got too much for some supporters as the Hammers' gallows humour resurfaced once more.

NAOMIM

Upton Park chief Terence Brown has promised supporters that the Hammers' sales are over after selling fans in the Bobby Moore Lower to Chelsea for £8m, despite claims he would only have to sell the fans in the Chicken Run. Brown had claimed in May that the 'nucleus' of West Ham support would be kept.

Brown's statement, released yesterday, read:

"Chelsea now have an array of talent on the field but because they have no fans, and the ones they do have are crap, when Roman came in and bid for some fans, I had to say yes – plus they were getting on my nerves a bit."

As the deal was sealed, those entering the Boleyn Ground for last night's game against Bradford were whisked down to Stamford Bridge in coaches and ordered to support Chelsea.

One former Hammers fan said:

"The board and I had been in discussions for 18 months about the renewal of my season ticket, but ultimately I just wanted Champions League football to further my enjoyment of the sport, something the club couldn't provide. So I've f****d off to Chelsea with the players."

Another supporter said: "I was preparing for life in Nationwide Division One when the board told me they'd sold me to Chelsea because their fans are so pony. But now I'm here, I'll forget about my past and start wearing naff earrings. Mind you, I've always supported Chelsea despite being an Upton Park regular for the last 30 years. As a young boy I used to stand on the terraces at Stamford Bridge and cheer on my favourite Blues such as Dennis Wise, Butch Wilkins, Charlie Cooke and Alan Dickens. In fact, I'm happy to kiss the badge just to prove it . . . there! Happy?"

Trevor Brooking insisted today that no more supporters would have to be sold, despite claims in a newspaper this morning that suggested some fans would be loaned out to Portsmouth 'till the end of the season.

However, a Portsmouth club source stated: "That's fiction, because even if we did, we'd have nowhere to put them, because our ground is a shit-hole."

Mr Brown was unavailable for comment today, as he had changed the £8m into five-pound notes and was rolling in the money in his garden.

BLAGG, today

Facing up to the new regime in Division One was going to be difficult. Would some of the better fringe players show their extra class in the lower league? Surely players such as Repka and Dailly would revel in their new found freedom away from predatory international strikers? The main question, though, concerned the now recovering Glenn Roeder. What would this young manager make of the situation after his serious illness?

Long-suffering fans of West Ham United were about to witness yet another twist in the bizarre saga.

Chapter 9

MANAGERIAL MERRY-GO-ROUND
Roeder-Sir Trev-Pardew – Season 2003-04

The start of the 2003-04 season was a strange affair. The club had been decimated in the fire sale following relegation and nobody was really sure what the future held. The squad still looked strong with David James in goal and Jermain Defoe up front, just two of the players expected to be sold, while players such as Tomas Repka, Christian Dailly and others were expected to show their extra class at the lower level.

A fit again Glenn Roeder had brought in a couple of players, notably Tottenham winger Matthew Etherington and ex-Wimbledon star striker David Connolly. These were reasonable signings whatever the position Hammers were in. Just before the first match, Roeder managed to gain the season loan of highly-rated Liverpool striker Neil Mellor and rumour was that the team coach had stopped off on the service station on the way to the first game at Preston to pick up the Anfield man who, presumably, was standing with his kit bag and a cardboard sign having travelled down from Liverpool.

Roeder then decided to play the tall Mellor up front with Defoe after barely a training session and a handshake with his new loan club. New striker Connolly was not happy and threatened to slap in a transfer request before even managing to locate a new locker. Roeder simply described Connolly famously as an 'Angry Ant' before bringing him on with the game tied at 1-1 at Deepdale on a hot August day. Inevitably, Connolly scored in spectacular fashion to cement a 2-1 win and the supporters scratched their heads and wondered.

A 0-0 home draw against fancied promotion contenders Sheffield United followed before the inevitable and much-feared trip to Rotherham at the end of the first month of the season. Trips to places like Millmoor were what every Hammers fan approached with curiosity. Would we turn on the style, puff our chests out and show we weren't afraid to slum it, or would we shrink like a salted snail and refuse to get involved?

Sadly it appeared to be the latter. Although territorially superior at times, the visitors seemed to lack a cutting edge and went behind after a quarter-an-hour to a goal the settled the match.

But worse was to follow when it was reported that the Hammers squad had refused to change in the Millmoor dressing rooms prior to the game due to their cramped and dilapidated state. Instead, went the report, they returned to their luxury hotel to get ready for the game.

Roeder later denied this had been the case but, whatever the truth of the matter, Rotherham manager Ronnie Moore made sure that his players believed it to be true, ensuring his team turned into a snarling, baying squad intent, just like Dad's Army's Corporal Jones, on "putting it up 'em". While the Sunday papers howled and Roeder protested the club's innocence, chairman Terence Brown decided that it was enough.

On the afternoon of Sunday, August 24, 2003, Glenn Roeder was sacked and nobody knew whether to laugh or cry. Three matches into the season and the manager had been sacked for losing a game. Had Brown and the rest of the board missed the previous nine months and suddenly woken, Rip Van Winkle style, to find out that we had been relegated and it wasn't good enough? You decide.

Whatever the answer, West Ham was now a laughing stock. Hanging onto a manager who barely merited a chance was one thing; supporting him in a serious illness was *another; but to then sack the same man just three matches into the season, and barely two weeks after finishing pre-season training following a summer convalescing, smacked of either gross incompetence or a staggering lack of sensitivity.*

BLAGG, Aug 2003

So it's farewell, Glenn Roeder. Relieved of his duties and the poisoned chalice he had been carrying for just over two seasons, we say goodbye to a man who never entirely convinced from Day One. He probably gave us his best and I think it's fair to say, from most of us here at Online, we gave our best in return. But sometimes unpalatable truths have to be said and this is such a time.

Glenn Roeder is undoubtedly an honest and reputable man. His coaching skills are seemingly recognised by many of his fellow managers and I've no doubt that his heart and soul were rooted firmly in the West Ham tradition. Glenn's illness last season was extremely unfortunate and there is not a Hammers fan in the world that wishes him further poor health. But . . .

The fact is that Roeder was a poor choice to replace Harry Redknapp as West Ham boss and his inept management skills were almost entirely responsible for West Ham's relegation last season. Roeder should have gone last November when it was patently obvious that he had 'lost' the dressing room and there was still time to for someone else to turn things around.

Terence Brown's inability to see this and his continuing support of Glenn Roeder was an appalling lack of judgement and, in the eyes of myself and most other fans, both men are responsible for the total dismantling of one of the finest squad of players ever to be assembled at Upton Park.

The finger of blame does not entirely point to Roeder, though. As I have opined before and at great length, the rot started with 'Mannygate', followed by the sale of Rio Ferdinand. The complete waste of the Rio fee and the subsequent loss of Frank Lampard were not of Roeder's doing. However, the rest of the mess is down to Glenn, I'm afraid, and it is only a sentimental fool who says otherwise.

Put simply, if we were to replay last season's matches

against West Brom, Birmingham, Bolton and Fulham at home, with any other Premiership manager in charge, would we still only have two points to show for it?

In retrospect, Roeder's seventh placed finish in 2001-02 did not do West Ham any favours. In fact, there were many alarm bells ringing during that season, particularly in defence where our away record was as bad as any in the Football League.

Undoubtedly, the club's inability to sign anyone to bolster a poor rearguard was considered crucial in the 2002-03 season and although Terence Brown's long pockets were the main reason, there's a real feeling that a stronger manager would have made some better decisions as to how to counteract the board's inability or reluctance to spend. As we now know, the early jettisoning of Joe Cole while there was still a buoyant transfer market may have made a lot of difference.

Of course, this being football, many questions remain. What exactly had Glenn done to warrant the sack after three matches in charge this season when he managed to go six months without a home win last? Has Brown played a crafty card to divert fans' wrath away from himself? And being as Roeder was such a surprise choice last time, when no one seemingly (and mysteriously) wanted the job, what is the chance of getting someone decent in this time?

Wrongly or rightly I felt my spirits rise when I heard we were looking for a new manager. So will it be for the better? All this can be debated in the days (or probably, this being West Ham, months ahead). In the meantime, prepare yourself for more stormy stories in the real *Eastenders* script that the BBC bosses rejected as being too preposterous. .

Talking of which . . . is Alfie Moon available?

Gutted Hammer
Yesssssssssssssssssssssssssssssssss! At last!

Ouest Jambonnier
Look guys, the fact remains, when HR was not offered a new contract we all knew the board just wanted a 'yes man' in so that they could dismantle the squad. They got that and now we're in Division One. GR was never going to do

anything special – he was looked at by many senior members of the squad as a nobody. In the end that filtered to rest of the squad and that's what started the whole ball rolling off down the hill. Thank the board for not employing a stronger, more experienced person.

Tynan

Roeder wasted money just as well as Redknapp. James is a good keeper but given the weaknesses we had in defence, should he have been bought?

I cannot remember how much money Roeder had available to spend when he took over, but say it was £11m, and he spent £3.5m on DJ, then one-third of his budget went on a position that was not our weakest area. Doesn't seem too clever to me.

What if that money had been spent on a top class central defender? Given DJ's moments of madness, along with Repka's, I think some might question whether they were in fact good buys.

Anonny

You think James is a bad buy? The now England keeper? Shaka was rapidly losing it when James signed. How many world-class saves has James made for us? Shaka was dooont, Jamoo io, woll, world olaoo.

Show me a manager who hasn't made a bad buy. I think Roeder's stands up well alongside others. Even Winterburn was good for a season and would have been better if he was prepared to stay in position and not go gallivanting.

The problem with Roeder was he lost the dressing room.

Ouest Jambonnier

I don't believe the loss of form and enthusiasm shown by the likes of Sinclair, Kanouté and Di Canio was down to losing the dressing room. The more mature players knew that the man had no idea, and then the team lost direction.

Some of his buys have been OK, but some I still think are very dubious. I agree with the James conundrum. Why buy him when we had a decent keeper anyway and that money could have been used to bolster our weakest area – i.e. defence? It's all about priorities, which is all about management.

(Vladimir) Labant was also very dubious. Roeder was prepared to let Winterburn go at the end of the first season, then had to make an embarrassing U-turn when he realised Labant could not defend. Connolly and Brevett have been good buys but even a trained monkey cannot get everything wrong.

Waily

I think the Roeder timing is odd but can't say I'm too sorry, to be truthful. Regarding Labant, though – I actually feel sorry for managers in this respect. The bloke's a Czech international and I think Roeder had a right to expect that he might be useful. But then he arrives and can't find a house or his kids don't settle in a Chigwell school, or his wife wants to go back to Peruvia or somewhere, and all of a sudden it's the manager's fault. Short of buying all our players from Wimbledon, what can you do? Bloody hell, Joey Beauchamp couldn't settle on the other side of the M25!

Tynan

Losing the dressing room was just about the only thing Glenn didn't do. The players remained committed despite the awful performances.

Roeder's chronic failing for me is his tactical awareness and coaching of tactics, etc. We were turned over time and again by teams that countered our tactics or changed formations to exploit our weaknesses. Playing players out of position was an extension of that.

I'm not suggesting all his buys have been bad but I do question his priorities. We had a good enough team to stay up last year; everyone said so at the time, given proper managing. So on that basis I would say that Roeder was to blame. TB allowed him the tools to avoid relegation at least.

Pin-Up

I'd love to see what PDC would do at the club. Maybe not as manager, but at least as a player-coach

Confused Hammer

Why the f*** would anybody want PDC involved in the coaching? – too stupid to even comment on.

KIDDERS
I would, and I'm not stupid. Did you actually watch the guy play football or were you too busy reading *The Sun*, believing all their stories?

AdelaideHammer
What about Tony Cottee? I reckon he could do the job OK.

Ironphilly
Ladbrokes have apparently stopped taking bets on Nigel Winterburn. Surely, even Terence Brown wouldn't do that to us

South Sydney Hammer
There's a bloke called Harry at Portsmouth who has been described by some as managing his teams like a second-hand car dealer manages his showroom, but his team is top of the Premiership. Maybe he would consider a move to a big club like West Ham United . . .

Paddy Hammer
How can anyone seriously see PDC cutting it as West Ham manager? Personally, I'd be happy to see Bryan Robson get the job – he managed to get Boro promoted and to a couple of Cup finals. I know many do not like him but I'd still have him over the inexperienced Dowle and (Stuart) Pearce. Perhaps Dowle as assistant to Robson?

Hotplates Davis
Pop Robson is coming back?

Frank White
Dowie will get it.

Tibbsy
The odds on Ray Lewington have reduced from 14/1 to 8/1 today. Are we not big enough to attract/employ a

manager with at least some level of success in top-flight football?

KIDDERS

OK, so we all agree Roeder was a mistake, let's now worry who's next. DOWIE? (No different to Roeder), GODDARD? (No), ROBSON? (No, Just imagine watching Middlesbrough), PEARCE? (No), CURBISHLEY? (What makes you think he'll manage us now?) GRAHAM (Couldn't afford his salary). Many other candidates have been thrown into the hat but none stand out for me. Can't help but think that DOWIE will get it. I'm still for PDC meself!

Tacchini kid

That sacking was as inevitable as night following day.

Glenn has at last been saved from further humiliating both himself and the club. It's sad that a decent man was placed in such an unfortunate position in the first place (reminds me of Graham Taylor and the England job) – a man so patently out of his depth that it became embarrassing to watch. No clear leadership skill, poor decision-making, lack of motivational skills coupled with a disastrous failure to 'build from the back' left us in this awful situation.

I guess the way forward in the short to medium term must be to unite behind the team and really give Trev and the lads a real lift, like Hammers fans can. However, we must not forget that what has happened here is that we have been thrown a sacrificial lamb . . . and we ought not to forget whose decision it was to appoint Glenn Roeder in the first place.

WestHam Family

How sad. It was good to be a supporter a few seasons back – a great team, a great tradition and, very often, beautiful football. Some of Di Canio and Kanouté's goals were pure magic. But the whole thing became unravelled and our golden squad gradually got sold off and never gelled into the team that could, theoretically, have won some decent silver. The board did not even do a good job of marketing such a great club – it was all allowed to go to the wall. The golden opportunity with lads who came through the ranks has gone and every time I see Chelsea on TV and see "our three players" it makes me sick. I watched Rio make a sensational tackle in the last two minutes at Newcastle. Pure, pure talent and superb timing in the penalty box. Such a waste.

South Sydney Hammer
Nice one, Mr Blagg. I agree with all that you say and I would add that I think the club did Glenn Roeder a tremendous disservice by appointing him manager when he clearly lacked the credentials to do the job.

Not only has this damaged the club we love, but it's probably irreparably damaged Glenn's chances of landing any job in football again. I am as glad as anyone that Glenn is gone but I do feel sorry for him, as it always seemed that this was inevitable given his lack of experience in the top flight.

Bubblehead
Roeder should never have got the job in the first place. I do not wish him any harm as a person, but due to the board's incompetence and his own belligerence and his own incompetence, they destroyed the best team we have had for two decades. Now the board should go and let's pray we get some people in who want to build our club into a real force.

Claret Hoop
On what basis do some people keep on saying that Glenn was "an excellent coach"?

Where did he ever demonstrate that he had a good tactical nous? Was there a single match in the last 18 months where you can honestly say that West Ham were purring? Think about it . . .

Brooking showed more savvy and guile in three difficult matches than Roeder did in a whole season (and two pre-seasons. Good piece as ever, Billy.

Trevor Brooking's Claret 'N' Blue Army
Yikes, and the days when we were looking for a new manager and got Roeder seem to me like they happened

only yesterday. Stuart Pearce's name has been mentioned. A hard man for a hard job? And I think there will be open riots if Paul Goddard gets the job.

How Now Brown Cow
One down and the board to go.

Roeder couldn't even see, or worse, was too proud to admit, why Ronnie Moore would have taken advantage of the changing room *faux-pas*. Doesn't he know that the other side might want to win and man-management is all about geeing people up to achieve more than is expected? Anyway, this doesn't matter now.

Decision made on Roeder makes sense: they've been able to sell all the players they wanted, a couple of games in is not too late to make a recovery and not too early – i.e. we know you are sick but we are firing you anyway.

We all know that the board believe in counting pennies and that debt is a terrible thing, but most of the country lives with debt throughout their life – not only managing to live with it, but making significant progress, too. For us mere mortals it's called a mortgage.

Fingers crossed that the people who can show their money and, if they need a few quid from me to do it, all they need to do is ask.

Distraught Hammer
This had to be the plan all along. They couldn't have brought in another manager at the end of last season, then sold off all those players – he wouldn't have stood for it. So the plan was, keep Roeder in charge while the squad is dismantled to pay for the mess of getting relegated, then wait and see what happens at the start of the season. Three wins, or two wins and a draw, and everyone is happy. A new manager couldn't have done better.

But a sign of continuing mess – not surprising considering Roeder barely had enough players to pick a side from – and out Roeder goes. The new man comes in with the best young squad in the country already sold off and starts with a clean slate.

Unfortunately it could be the club that suffers for the unprofessional way that this happened as promotion, though by no means impossible, gets more and more tricky the longer the club goes without stability.

Roeder was sold down the river, left with no squad two days before the start of the season – then is expected to keep winning. While Roeder took the club down, I think he's been treated appallingly since then. He's been used.

irisiris
Hutchison was player-of-the-year for Sunderland on the right side of midfield. He doesn't play well there because he is sulking – he thinks he should play in the middle. In fact I've got a suspicion that on top of the lure of a silly salary and a move down south, he was also promised a move to centre-midfield. So, in truth, he may have some cause to be disgruntled but the fact that he is paid shit loads of money, has had a year off with injury and won't get an opportunity anywhere else, should ensure that he shows some professionalism. To put in performances like he has down in the first division is a disgrace and one of the few things I don't blame Roeder for.

Generally, injuries, changing in hotels and everything else aside, Roeder should have been sacked solely for the team he put out on the park on Saturday. How, in three weeks, he could select Repka at CB, RB and then LB smacks of utter incompetence and provides ample justification for getting rid of him.

HOK
If it is to believed that Roeder is a great coach and accepted that he is also a crap manager, then the board can now add the loss of a great coach to their list of mistakes, given that Glenn would have been more than happy to remain in the backroom staff had another manager been appointed.

highbury hammer
I am glad to see Glenn go but also believe it's the TB side-step in action here. A battle won but the war still continues.

ThE iCe CrEaM BoY
I think it was a woeful decision to give Glenn the job in the first place. Well out of his depth, he was left to drown in his

own shortcomings. That said, we have to remember Glenn is an excellent coach and I, for one, wish him well in his pursuit of another coaching job. The guy has determination and guts and if his ability as a manager was matched by those two virtues, he would be a great boss. Unfortunately for Glenn and us, that isn't so.

The board's option to do things on the cheap and general incompetence is the root cause of all of WHU's ills. They could have had Alan Curbishley two years back but chose to muck him about. You have to remember the old adage: 'cheap is dear'.

I think Glenn was treated pretty shabbily, being kept on as the presiding manager whilst the fire sale was conducted. Glenn should have gone last year when it was patently obvious he wasn't up to the job. But we know who the real enemies of WHU are and that should always be remembered.

I feel sorry for Glenn because he should never have been put in the position he was in. Someone should have relieved him of his duties last year because Glenn, being a proud man, wasn't going to quit. Then again, you know what they say: pride comes before a fall.

Clack

I suspect the timing was to do with Roeder's disgraceful behaviour on Saturday when he truly shamed our club and left Brown with no choice but to dismiss him. The more I here about Saturday, the worse it gets. It now turns out that Roeder had planned getting half-changed and prepared in the hotel beforehand.

I hope the club also sack the psychologist, the fitness trainer, open up the training ground to the fans again and go back to playing some off-the-cuff attacking football, the West Ham way, and we can get our club back again from this crackpot and his cranky new age ideas

Alex x

"What exactly had Glenn done to warrant the sack after three matches in charge this season when he managed to go six months without a home win last?" ...well, the answer was plainly obvious last autumn when we played utter crap time and time again, even with guys like Cole, Defoe, PDC, Sinclair in the team.

GOOD RIDDANCE. Thank God this decision has come early this season

Watching England midweek and then Chelsea and Man Utd this weekend dominating the Premier League with "our products", just made me so depressed that this club has let an incredible opportunity slip. The sale of Rio was a disaster for WHUFC. We had a great team with Lampard, PDC, Cole, Kanouté, etc, until our board decided we was a feeder club.

inconsistant fc

Now the debate turns to who's next? I'd love to see Trevor take over full-time. He will organise the squad but also attract other players of quality. Dowie did a good job at Oldham last season but is he really the man to take us straight up again? We need a true West Ham figurehead at the helm and Trevor will give them all a good kick up the arse and keep the fans happy.

I now think that we will claim our rightful place and be back in the Premiership as champions.

Selektah

Agreed Bill, spending the precious Lampard money on Hutch was a disaster. Repka, a disaster. Glenn couldn't motivate or man-manage senior players. It's 10 months too late but what sweet music to my ears.

Swiss Toni

Got it right on as usual. Especially with the piece about not getting rid of Roeder in Nov. 2002. That's my main gripe.

Woody

Can't help but agree it would seem that he had lost the dressing room. James indicated as much in an interview yesterday. James tends to talk a lot of sense and he seems to me to be saying that the team could see the cracks appearing, yet Roeder didn't? The team do not seem to be that worried by his departure. He was also very expansive in his praise of Trevor Brooking. I hope Geno takes it on full-time.

Paulo Di Godio

Can't agree that everything after Lampard is Glenn's fault. When you have a house of cards and remove the first couple from the bottom, is it really the fault of the new man that the rest comes tumbling down?

The fault lies with the board. They engineered Rio's sale, sacked Redknapp knowing that Lampard would then leave. Replaced Redknapp with the cheapest option. Glenn was that option and I truly believe he did his very best – but with someone behind him (dagger in hand), he never had a chance.

Alex V

That just about sums up the disaster perfectly.

mallard

Forget the joke – Alfie Moon would have the charisma we have lost since Harry left. Plus he has a better line in shirts.

HAMMERDOWNUNDER

Well said, Billy. I am overjoyed! When I walked into the pub this afternoon to hear of Roeder's sacking, it was music to my ears. it's probably a year too late but better late than never. Bring on George Graham – if anyone can take a two bob squad and turn it into glory, it is him. Ask Steffen Freund. The geezer's got a Cup winners' medal – and we know how good he is!

Gutted Hammer

Robson? Lewington? Winterburn? Moore?
Noooooooooooooooooooooooooooooo...

BLAGG, today

In fact Alfie Moon was available but the man himself suggested the club turn back to the God-like genius of Trevor Brooking. The England man was happy to take charge on a temporary basis but made it clear that he didn't want it full time. The search for a new boss was on again.

My own football career mounted to an ill-fated season-and-a-half as manager in charge of Mooro's Second XI, the team from Bobby Moore's own pub on Stratford Broadway. This would be a much better tale if I could regale you of stories of Bobby popping over to Wanstead Flats on a Sunday morning and giving me tips on organising a flat back four. But sadly, there are no such magical tales. My only sight of the great man was when the team went back to the pub on Sunday lunchtimes after matches – usually to discuss who was to blame for the latest 6-1 debacle – only to see our mentor supping pints and demolishing peanuts at the end of the bar.

I wish now I had approached him and asked him for advice. Even if he'd said: 'Yeah, stop managing my bloody pub team, you're making me a laughing stock', it would have been something. As it is, now I can only look back in wonder at those times.

Can you imagine popping into your local pub now and seeing, say, David Beckham sitting on a stool watching TV with barely anyone saying anything to him? Yet here was a man who had won a European trophy, an FA Cup and – gulp – a WORLD CUP (eat your heart out, Beckham) and he sits in your local and is only bothered by the time it takes to top up his lager glass and open up a pack of Percy Dalton's.

But I digress. With few takers on the managerial front I thought it only right to apply for the vacant post. I had just spent six months out of work and I was sure my asking rate wouldn't trouble Terence Brown too much. Sadly, my application never even warranted a reply.

BLAGG, Sept 2003

The problem with such earth-shattering Hammers events as relegation, managerial sackings and appointments is that I feel duty bound to comment even when there's really not much that can be said that hasn't already found its way into print.

On five separate occasions this week I've read that the frontrunner for the vacant hot seat at Upton Park is Hart/Graham/Pardew/Dowie/Robson (delete as applicable) and the real truth in the claims only depend on which newspaper you prefer. In fact, the only name not mentioned among the 40 'serious' contenders (does this mean they discount WHO message board contributors?) is that of yours truly, William H. Blagg Esq. I threw my hat into the ring just hours after Glenn was sent away with a flea in his ear and I still reckon I represent Terence Brown's only real alternative to the usual hoopla of former failed favourites and untested wannabes.

I'll grant my season tenure in charge of Mooro's back in the 70s wasn't my finest spell in football but I've learned a lot about management since then and at least I have a couple of Hugo Boss suits and a chin. I reckon I have what it takes to shine in front of a TV camera and I could at least provide the odd sound bite or two. Hopefully, I might even be able to provide the merry quip that will find its way into the hearts of the nation in much the same way as those words of wisdom from the previous incumbents at Upton Park.

Are there any of us out there who haven't perused our chequebooks over the past few years and declared ourselves 'down to the bare bones'? And only last week, after Lady B had angrily thrown sausages at me following a particularly nasty spat, I had cause to refer to her as an 'angry ant'. These are the type of things that the fans expect from the boss at Upton Park and I believe I can provide them.

I'm free any day next week, Terry.

Beyond that, of course, we have the usual sorry tales of people making a prat of themselves as they try to distance/ingratiate themselves from the vacancy that everyone in football wants. As long as I have been watching football – and that's 108 years now – there has always been a pecking order. Do you remember how aggrieved we all were when Rio Ferdinand joined Leeds? A club that – we claimed correctly – was no bigger than our own? How many of us stifled a guffaw when Rio eventually legged it to Old Trafford where his skills should have exported themselves to in the first place? We know we're not an Arse, Liverpool or ManUre. The fact that we are not a Chelsea or a Newcastle is a grating fact that we have to live with currently – particularly those of us who remember Tommy Langley at Stamford Bridge or David Kelly down at the Toon.

However, we also know West Ham United is a bigger club than Charlton or Reading, Crystal Palace and Millwall and no amount of swagger or bravado will convince any sensible person otherwise.

To explain this phenomenon to opposing supporters isn't easy, as it strikes hard at the very root of what supporting a club is all about. However, the fact is, if we remove ourselves from the intimacy of our own club, the same rules still apply. For example, picture if you will a Sheffield Wednesday supporter being told by a Reading fan some 10 years ago that, by 2003, they would be 'a bigger club'. You may look at the league table now and opine that the Reading supporter may be worth considering when picking your lottery numbers this week. But it don't work like that!

Wednesday is a bigger club (and I have no relationship with the Owls at all) and always will be. Sure, they are in a mess now but they will be back – and no amount of millionaires and Madejski stadiums can detract from that fact. Their 'size' is determined by a century of history for the club itself and the stadium and is built into the very fabric of the Hillsborough ground, its supporters and the area It represents.

In other words, if Alan Pardew is the man for the Hammers job (and I have no feeling one way or the other), then relative success at the Berkshire club is not the criteria. If you interview a James or try to tempt a new Cole then Upton Park is where you need to be to do it. To get to the top of the management tree you have to climb up and WHU are nearer to where the best conkers are. If you're more comfortable sitting in the chair in sunny Berks or slimy South London, then you're either:

1. Waiting for an even better offer (in which case you might like to consider if you're not over-reaching yourself) or...

2. You're not up to the job in the first place. Some might say loyalty should be a third option but at that I'll just have a bloody good laugh and remind you that this is professional football we're talking about here.

I know some of you are going to ask who I think should do the job and I can understand it if you feel a little cheated if I don't answer directly. But all I can do is direct you to a column I wrote about two seasons ago before Glenn Roeder was appointed. Being manager of West Ham United is a big job and demands a top man. I prefer someone who has stature, someone who has been there and done it. A proven force that can instil direction, discipline and attract players (particularly important for foreign imports).

If that were a George Graham or a Bryan Robson, then I wouldn't complain. I wouldn't mind a 'new Bill Shankly', like Alan Pardew, providing we're sure that the man is up to the job. I'm uncomfortable with honest scufflers who have done well with smaller outfits, so I'm not looking at a Ronnie Moore type. Similarly, I've been praying for years that we get away from the 'happy family' game that Iain Dowie or Stuart Pearce represent (I was a fairly lonely voice suggesting that Curbishley wasn't the right option last time).

I really need strong convincing that Paul Hart is a step-forward from Glenn Roeder and, if we start going down the Ray Lewington route then I'm gonna get myself a big gun and personally blow a hole in one of the turrets. That is not an option.

The key issue for me is for West Ham United to be represented by a big man. Someone who can win us matches. Someone who can handle the media while possessing the tactical acumen to deal with any crisis that the playing side can throw up. A person with an aura that can attract established top players while instilling confidence into younger names who want to break through into the big time. We need someone who looks equally as good in a suit as a tracksuit.

Do we know of anyone? Yeah, we do! Unfortunately, that man seems more interested in sitting next to John Motson in Tbilisi or bantering with the Walkers Crisps Kid.

So, it's out with the application forms. Prepare the human resources psychologist and get him to look out for those little tics. It's managerial merry-go-round time and West Ham just have to get it right this time. But then didn't we say that last time?

The fans, of course, had their own ideas of who should be the new boss . . .

Miss G
Well, I didn't make the short list, even though I have brought silverware back to my school this year on more than

one occasion.

Hotplates Davis

I don't think taking in your Grandmother's old cutlery into a
'Show and Tell' Primary class counts, Miss G! Although with
Terence Brown, who can tell?

doomhunk

Doesn't it irk anyone else that we went up behind
Newcastle 10 years ago and, despite outplacing them in the
PL for a couple of seasons, are right back where we started
while they have been having flirtations, although admittedly
ill-fated, with the Champions League? Do we really think that
Pardew is the right man to rectify this? Indeed, can it be
rectified? I will certainly get behind AP, but believe Brooking
is the man for the job. There must be something seriously
wrong behind the scenes if he cannot be persuaded to
overcome the family issues that seem to be preventing him
from taking the job on a full-time basis

Eric Minnesota USA

No mention of El Tel? The former Dagenham boy should
be worth the risk. After all, it would be a challenge for him
rather than sitting in the booth.

clack

The big man who fits all the criteria you mention is John
Toshack but, for some reason that I can't fathom, he's just
not being mentioned.

Maybe that's 'cos he's not considered a realistic option –
he's just doing a bit of TV pundit work at present, waiting for
the Barca or Liverpool job to come up?

I don't know but if WHU really are the big club you speak
of, Blagg, then surely an approach to Toshack should be
made.

West of London

I seem to remember that in the WHO article you wrote in
the pre-Roeder manager hunt two years ago, Blagg, you
said that the new man should have won something. Other
than Brooking, have the Pardews, Dowies and Moores won

anything?

It's boring, but it's true. Brooking scored the winner in the 1980 FA Cup final. The team are unbeaten under his leadership, because the players respect him and listen to what he tells them. If Terence Brown wants to do one good thing in this miserable life he has made for himself and 40,000+ others, he will make Trevor an offer he can't refuse, protect his broadcasting career, and appoint whoever Trevor needs to run the ship in his absence. Forget Pardew and the others. We've already got the solution to all our problems sipping sherry in the boardroom.

D.Rollo

Nicely observed, Blagg – until you get to that piece when we mention the names of Mr Graham and Mr Robson. "Instil direction, discipline and attract players"? What evidence is there that either of these has all these attributes? Both of them are a laughing stock in the game . . . Robson: open chequebook and a relegated squad filled with prima donnas and ill feeling. Graham: a worse record at Spurs than Christian Gross. I should add, though, that I am in nothing less than complete harmony with Mr Blagg re. Hart, Lewington and Moore, etc.

Why are people happy to tout these names without looking beyond the fact that they are only 'names'? They offer nothing we need. Why go backwards when we can go forwards?

The risk of bringing in a Dowie or (as seems 99% certain) a Pardew is far less than chancing our club on these dinosaurs of the modern game. Football has changed since Graham last had success in the league. Robson lacks so many necessary qualities.

By the way, Blagg, I'd suggest that your lone voice re. Curbs should probably have stayed hushed!
(BB: Spot on, Rollo)

Tricky Dev

Holes in the turrets, now there's a media event!

Kevin in Nova Scotia

Nice one, BB. I suspect Brooking would want a new

contract to put up with all that goes with a manager's life. Perhaps that is the linchpin? In that Trev is hung up on not losing the fans' love if things go sour.

Ronald_antly

What's all this tosh about needing to look good in a suit? If he looks good in a suit, fine, but all I care about is his ability to inspire the players to want to do the job for West Ham. He could prowl the touchline naked for all I care! Why do people think Robson is such a messiah? His last job ended with him having to get a man in to sort things out for him.

Nemesis

When you get that gun, Blagg, drop me a line and I'll help you blow a bloody big hole in BOTH of those stupid turrets.

dave

Trev should stay a director but accept a hands-on role for the year and drop most of his media work until Euro 2004. Bring in Stuart Pearce as manager. This man can inspire – he's had everything the players need. The fans will roar for him, and we can all see what effect that has on our results if we look at last season and the start of this. That's the deal.

Paddy Hammer

Sir Billy of Blagg – another quality article. Good work, mister! I know I've said it before, but the man for the job is Bryan Robson. He has experience, respect and will get those lazy feckers in the squad working. He even knows how to attract flair players (Junihno, Ravanelli, etc) and get them to work their nuts off.

Terminator 2

I hate to say it but all you ***** who said over the last few years that Rodent, TB, et al were OK have NO right to start criticising the selection process of the new manager, or even suggest who he/she should be, because you obviously ain't got a clue. I don't have a clue either, as all the people I would suggest would cost at least £5.00 an hour and TB isn't going to pay that unless all you say is YES, YES, YES!
Trevor is the man, and if he really cares about the club

then he will take on the job for the (and longer hopefully) year and ask Stuart Pearce or GG to help. Whatever happens, I just hope and pray that maybe someday we chose someone who has the club's future at heart and give that person some real dosh to buy some decent players (or keep them) and support the future of the club. Oh, by the way Julian Dicks is the man 4 me.

Johnny The Web

One name that hasn't been touted much – Christian Gross. Seriously, I'd go for either an Alan Pardew or Iain Dowie as Team Coach with Trevor as Director of Football looking after them. Or I'd go for George Graham. I think he would get us out of the Nationwide - who says it has to be pretty?

out now, brown cow

It being the 21st century, how about being the first club to have a woman manager? I agree, BB, that they would have to have stature, look equally good in a suit or a track-suit, attract the top stars as well as instil confidence in the younger players trying to break through into the big time, and would be able to handle the media. Anybody know anyone fits the bill?

alfs barnet

Another masterpiece from Blagg. Well done. I'd back you for the job.

BLAGG, today

Fan comments can often go to show just how diverse opinions are on footballing moments of great pith and gravity. In this case those who wanted to court the attentions of Alan Pardew eventually got their way.

Pardew was a former Crystal Palace and Charlton Athletic journeyman player who had gained a lot of attention with Reading, leading them to the upper reaches of the First Division from the depths of the Second.

Hardly a fashionable club, with Pardew at the helm and millionaire chairman John Madejski holding the reins, Reading had become a bright, forward thinking franchise. Pardew's coaching skills were highly regarded and he was viewed as being one of the up and coming breed of new, young English managers.

West Ham obviously had a view of where they wanted to go. As with Alan Curbishley a year earlier, there was a sense that the club had decided on their man from the off. Terence Brown approached Reading seeking permission to speak to Pardew but Madejski, turned them down flat.

This time, though, Pardew was obviously flattered by the offer and, denied the opportunity to even speak to West Ham, he resigned as manager of Reading and went on gardening leave while the clubs tried to resolve his position.

Brooking agreed to step back in as caretaker manager in the meantime but there was a feeling that the team was suffering under the constant speculation and upheaval. Results were reasonable but patchy. Eventually, Pardew was given the job as West Ham manager officially and the next era began in October 2003.

Pardew took up his post in a lively fashion, trying to ingratiate himself with the fans with his references to the Academy, World Cup-winning heroes and promises to return West Ham to its rightful place among the big boys.

Fans were to learn later that the new manager, who liked to be known as 'Pards', was fond of a football soundbite or three.But, initially, Pardew's introduction was sufficient enough for Blagg to opine that he 'liked the cut of his jib'.

Trevor Brooking, the best manager West Ham never had, was eventually lured away from Upton Park to become an influential and much-respected Director of Football Development for the FA.

He received a knighthood in 2004 for his services to football. This was added to the one that Blagg awarded him in May 1980.

Don Watts
Pardew ain't got it for me – looks like Roeder, only worse. Another bad decision from the board.

Steadmania
I'm optimistic about Pardew. I like the way he signed (Hayden) Mullins and told him he's wasting his time at

Palace. Roeder couldn't motivate the best team we had in years. The fans need to see players earning their money and being told if they're not. Where did Brian Deane come from, though? Those kind of signings scare me.

StR

It's difficult to see why anyone would have wanted someone with West ham connections for the job. The only one who has had any success at all is John Lyall, so there is no reason to believe that provides any advantage whatsoever.

Claret Hoop

Have to agree with the sentiment of the piece. Basically, I think we have captured the best manager that we could have hoped to . . . and that we'll definitely be back where we belong in the not too distant future.

Let's not forget that as well as Lou 'make-mine-an-each-way' Macari, our greatest manager ever – Ron Greenwood – was a non-West Ham man as well.

Captain_Flashman

I just hope he gets the room to really change the attitude of the club; we've started to look extremely outmoded of late. Chips with everything, 'win-or-lose on the booze!' I didn't mind too much until it became 'lose and lose and lose on the booze'.

strong dreams

I believe that our team's efforts to date this season have been hampered by injury, management changes and new players not having the time or structure to fit in . . . and we are still there or thereabouts. If Pardew is the man some suggest (and his jib is indeed cut in an attractive way), the first half of the season has been a warm up and we are about to go on the mother of all winning sprees.

The Joker

I wish I had a jib like Alan's.

Snailsy

Can I be the first to sing? Chim Chimeney, Chim Chimeney Chim Chim Pardew? OK, I'll get my coat . . .

Ol Blue Eyes

BB, I agree that AP looks good. But was intrigued by your question about would WHU have stayed up if Roeder had been hospitalised the month before and Brooking had been In charge then?

In fact I looked at the previous eight games before Brooking took over and Roeder's record was: 4 wins, 3 draws, 1 defeat. Can't see your point.

marky ironworks 1895

The cut of Pardew's jib is perfect. Just perfect.

marky ironworks 1895

Oops! I posted the "The cut of Pardew's jib is perfect" reply before I spotted we had signed Brian Deane. His jib is now slightly suspect.

Senor Coconut

Now I'm not usually one for irrational exuberance but I think we might just be OK with this bloke. I like the cut of his jib, too.

Baron von Evilswine

I think most of us share your optimism, BB. Mind you, going from the worst ever WH manager in living history to what appears to be the best, just doesn't seem the West Ham way. It's like being released from an insane asylum to be told your Nan has left you a million in pools money.

Provided we can keep Pards sweet, the sky really is the limit for us (give or take a couple of years).

Aussie Mike

Well written, balanced article – but please can we file this one away for 12 months' time for a review.

Sutton soul hammer

Like what I've seen of AP so far. Agree, too, that he says all the right things and I don't hold my head in shame anymore when the TV boys 'cross live to the West Ham manager' . . .

Thirsty

I was sitting in a box just behind Pardew last night and watched him soak up the pressure on the touchline, his feet either within inches of the technical line or actually over it.

There were six or so Lucozade bottles on the floor next to him and he was constantly drinking from them throughout the match. During the second half he was drinking a hot tea/coffee, eyes constantly on the game and shouting instructions and encouragement. Really focussed and controlled nervous excitement. Totally different to Roeder's animated conversations with Paul Goddard, pen and paper in hand. The man inspires confidence and I feel if anyone can motivate the players and get the team back into the Premiership, he can.

TCS

Whenever he has been interviewed on Sky, I have looked forward to what he has to say and usually smiled at the end of it. He just seems to look like a manager to be proud of. With Roeder I was always faintly embarrassed.

Our Dave

"I like the cut of his jib". So do I, young Billy me lad, so do I. Three things make a winning team: Physical fitness, skill and mental ability. These are the things that Alan will bring to the club, especially the last of these. Say to ANY individual: "Hey, mate, you are doing a great job." or "That was a skilful thing you just did", then he/she will be motivated. Positive attitude always.

D.Rollo

A nice turn in optimism, and yep, it does feel good. All in all, nothing can ever go wrong ever again . . . probably. Even his jib.

Chapter 10

WHISTLE Down The Wind

Relegation and the sale of virtually all the 'crown jewels' left West Ham supporters bitter, upset and understandably angry. Questions were asked of the team and the manager but most of the bile was reserved for the board and, principally, chairman Terence Brown.

It was inevitable that the grumbling individuals would eventually form themselves into a collective whole and this took the form of the BROWN OUT and WHISTLE groups. Both collectives have the same aim: to oust the current board (or at least make it more accountable) while calling for the resignation of Brown for presiding over arguably the worst period in the club's history.

Allegations of financial mis-management and asset-stripping were (and still are) endemic, with the fan web sites full of claim and counter-claim. Although all fans had something to say about the continuing decline of the Hammers, suggestions of dubious company share dealings followed by legal and financial ramifications left a large number of fans confused

On a broader level, there is no doubt that the fact that many ex-West Ham players had moved across London to Chelsea, where Roman Abramovich was waving his millions, caused fans to glance enviously at the Blues while recalling similar financial excesses carried out by Sir Jack Hayward at Blackburn Rovers and even, to a lesser extent, John Madejski at Reading. Why did West Ham always appear to be selling to catch up without ever looking like getting near the leading pack?

One of the major issues for critics of the club structure is the alleged lack of accountability due to the club's share issue. Although West Ham United PLC claim strong support for their actions, critics point to the fact that less than 50 people control 87% of the shareholding – an estimated17.2 million shares out of a total of 20 million. As these shares are owned by the board themselves, their extended families and ex-directors, etc, with a further one million shares held by identified nominees, only two million shares are available to the public.

WHISTLE claimed that they had £20m pledged to them by anonymous investors willing to buy into the club via a share issue, if major club lenders like Barclays Bank helped to oust the current board. WHISTLE spokesman Mike Hanna was quoted as saying: "We're not proposing a takeover. We want a share issue that doubles the shares available in the company. Certain people have undertaken to buy certain amounts of those shares, and their money would be used to appease the debt."

However, Terence Brown, backed by a statement from Barclays, simply rubbished the claims that West Ham was in dire straits, and took legal action against the supporters representing WHISTLE by claiming they were undermining the club with spurious figures that had no basis in fact.

The battle continues in unseemly fashion . . .

BLAGG, Nov 2003

There are a number of problems with me tackling the thorny subject of Terence Brown, the board and the club's finances.

Firstly, is the alarming fact that the Blagger left Thomas Lethaby School for Young Offenders with nought but a Grade 5 CSE in Principles of Accounts. This was gained by turning up on the day and successfully managing to write my name in large red crayon across the top of the page. In fact, had I not dribbled while falling asleep on Page 2, then I may even have even been upgraded to level 4.

Subsequently, I cannot understand the club accounts and I make no attempt to repair this lack of knowledge. I have had emails that say: "It's quite easy, Blagger old boy, simply take this and that and compare it blah, blah, etc" but all that happens is I fall over and hit my head while trying to remove my socks, so that I can use my toes to count.

I'll admit I can barely distinguish a ledger from a hole in the ground and this lack of mathematical acumen means that I follow financial arguments with the heart rather than the head. In short, some people you like and trust; others you don't. As an example, it was very easy for me to side with Harry Redknapp against Terence Brown when the former was shown the door, as it was obviously Big Bad Terry against our own lovable rogue.

However, I then became concerned at the involvement of close relatives acting as agents on certain players who, with the best will in the world, appear to have a rather dubious recent history. A case could be made for the failure of Cameroon World Cup star Rigobert Song to cement his place in the Hammers rearguard. But Titi Camara? The man could barely walk and chew gum at the same time! It is inconceivable that someone thought this was a reasonable bid to make and if I accept that then my perceptions of the people involved must change.

As a result, I'm aware that not being privy to certain salient facts means that my judgement is impaired. It isn't that I don't care or that I'm being deliberately obtuse; it's simply a case that the arguments as to the validity of, for instance, buying back shares or being able to quote something at an AGM not in the Year End accounts, is a matter, frankly, beyond my ken.

Following on from this is the not insignificant fact that it has become apparent that legal action against supporters is not something our chairman is afraid to undertake. Paolo Di Cattio needs a roof over his whiskered head and if Lady Blagg hasn't got 10 cupboards to put her shoes in then my life isn't worth living.

So, if you don't mind, I'll just pass on whether or not Terence Brown failed to give WHISTLE the correct amount of time to add their protest into the minutes of the last AGM, and move swiftly on. Is that OK, Mr Brown, sir?

Where I do feel I can bring something to the debate, though, is in the area of common sense, acumen and general business sense. You see, despite my financial blind spot, I do have vast experience in looking after a small business (I have an accountant!) and the principles are the same. Like most fans, I don't give a fiddler's fart who is in charge of the club providing we have a nice ground and it is full of singing supporters cheering on a team that we can be proud of.

With regard to certain club matters, I can see that my perceptions are not always right or fair. For instance, I am aware that I am not in full control of the facts regarding transfers and contracts; nor am I aware of what happens on a day-to-day basis in the dressing room. So, if a player is disruptive and the other players won't talk to him – let's pick a player at random . . . oh . . . say, David Connolly, then the manager may well take an offer on him if a bid comes in. The manager obviously can't then say: "Look, I couldn't stand his angry ant attitude so I let him go". That would be unethical and unprofessional.

So all the fan sees is what seems like a good player leaving the club for a supposed rival. That's not the club being secretive; it's a business acting as it should do.

Nevertheless, there are areas where things need to be a bit more above board (ha!) because, if you're not then people can see for themselves and will ask pertinent questions. For example, if you have something that someone wants to buy for £18m and there is a good chance that you can get some good use out of that thing and may make a few hundred off the back of it, then people will ask questions if you decide to sell it. Particularly if you are well aware that hanging onto that object means that its value will increase anyway and any time over the next five years you can almost certainly sell that thing for £36m if you change your mind.

If you're not sure if the 'thing' is going to have a value or not, then you should get someone in who has a better feel for the commodity you are selling. Nothing wrong with delegating what you don't know or understand. I have an agreement with my accountant – I don't try and work out my VAT and he doesn't try and fix my PC. Seems to work well.

Similarly, if you are in grave danger of losing £100 if you don't spend £30, then you should have very good reasons for not doing it. There may be times when you lose money through no fault of your own and buy badly or sell at the wrong time, but you learn from this and try to ensure it doesn't happen again. If it continually happens over a long period of time then you may need to rethink what you are doing. Perhaps you may be better selling holiday homes.

The key factor to me, though, is attitude. If your business does lose a lot of money then it's not good enough to say: "Look, MHS and Microsoft lose money – it's our turn this week". That suggests a poor attitude, and stagnation, and inept decision-making at the top is not good for any business. But that is what all this is about. It's called the 'Peter Principle'.

The 'Peter Principle' is an excellent theory put forward by US psychologist and teacher, Lawrence J. Peter. The principle states that: 'In any hierarchy people will rise to their level of incompetence'. In short, if you are good at your job you will keep getting promoted to a point at which you are no longer able to give of your best. In a hierarchal structure you are rarely demoted back to do the job you could do, so every business is full of people who have reached their level of incompetence.

The only successful work being done is being carried out by those who haven't yet reached their level. If you're smart – and this is that common-sense and acumen part – you say 'I'm good at this so I'll stay doing it' or, better still, take the top job with all it's glory and salary and then make sure you populate beneath you with people who haven't reached their level of incompetence and can deal with the stuff you don't know about.

When arguments start up about the Rio Stand and the museum and the players who have left, I'm taken back to the series of West Ham forums that Peter Storrie used to run with Harry and some of the players at the old Rollerbowl in Collier Row, Romford in the late 90s. I was there one evening when someone asked about the development of Upton Park and the impact it could have on money being available for the squad; the old 'if we build it, they still won't come unless we have something decent in it' argument.

Storrie was quite adamant, the finance of the team and the rebuilding of the stadium should not impact on each other. The club had secured a large and very good interest-bearing loan for rebuilding because the real estate of the Boleyn Ground was a prize asset. No bank would mind lending money for building because they could never lose it. At worst, they could move in and reclaim the building and build a Tesco's on it.

I remember that night and I remember how we purred with pleasure. Trevor Sinclair, Shaka Hislop and Ian Pearce were there, too. None of them would need to go from the club to finance a new stand.

Was Peter Storrie lying? Or was he a man who hadn't reached his level of incompetence yet? We will never know because, although a sell-out, there were only a few hundred of us there that night. The tales of major shirt sponsors (a proposed, new South African airline? "We're just waiting for it all to take off" – laughter all round) and 'financial stability in our time' are now just heresay and conjecture and look as if they belong to the last century now (irony intended!).

So in conclusion, while I'm concerned that WHISTLE have almost as many questions to answer as Mr Brown, I'm grateful to anyone who throws stones into the stagnant pond that is the West Ham boardroom and thinks they may see things about which I have no knowledge.

Let's hope we have cause to remember the group for more than just turning off the light, pursing the lips and blowing...

Herts Hammer

West Ham United AGM - Whistle Objectives Achieved

Whistle – the group of West Ham United PLC – ("the company") shareholders behind a move to unseat the company's current board of directors have today reviewed the AGM of December 8, 2003.

The following salient points arise:

1. Whistle meeting objectives

Whistle's intent for the AGM was to raise the profile of the Whistle group, question the chairman, Mr Brown, on the failed business performance of West Ham United PLC and to establish a platform for the removal of Mr Brown and other associated directors in the near-term future. These objectives were achieved beyond expectations, with Mr Brown constantly defending himself against the pre-meeting Whistle statements on all aspects of the business performance, lack of ethics and invisible governance.

2. Legal position of Notice of Motion

Mr Brown opened the meeting by referring directly to the

Notice of Motion that Whistle had lodged with West Ham United PLC:

Whistle has received expert legal advice and retains its view that West Ham United PLC were acting under incorrect advice and that their actions could cause the meeting to be classed as null and void. However, Whistle takes the view that to enforce that position would achieve little and only cause disruption to the attending shareholders, many of whom had scheduled time away from work to attend the meeting. However, Whistle reaffirms its assurance that its notice of motion should have been included in the agenda of the AGM.

3. Unprofessional/Evasiveness of Mr Brown

Mr Brown continually failed to answer questions put to him, preferring to use evasive tactics ranging from avoidance to contradiction. As in the failure to answer the question put by Mike Hanna. Mr Brown was asked: "What can you say to shareholders has changed with the management of this business to convince the shareholders that the appalling business results of the last five years have been arrested and that we can expect improved business results in the future?" Mr Brown objected to Mr Hanna using current time information that came after the end of year results under discussion, (as of May 31, 2003) emphasising that we had to focus on the results to year-end May 31, 2003, but then placed no such restriction on himself and continually used information that came after May 31, 2003 to justify his answers.

4. Proxy Votes

Whistle is very disturbed that proxy votes, which had been correctly returned for their use, mysteriously failed to materialise prior to the meeting, in that West Ham United PLC's agents claimed to have no such records assigning these votes to the Whistle representative.

5. Voting Results

West Ham United PLC claimed strong support for their motions, the facts though do not stand up well to scrutiny.

Less than 50 people control 87% of the shareholding, (17.2 million shares out of a total of 20 million shares). These are, the board themselves, their extended families and ex-directors and their families. Furthermore, one million shares are held by identified nominees, making only two million shares available to the public.

A significant number, in excess of one million shares, of the supposed secured shareholding, abstained, which certainly indicates a less than confident endorsement of the annual results or the motions as voted on.

6. Next Steps

Whistle wishes to make clear that their focus is, and remains, the improvement of the business management of West Ham United PLC through placement of suitably qualified and experienced individuals to replace Mr Brown and his failing business associates.

These steps will take some time as confidence must be built with the respective business parties and credibility further enhanced to ensure that all the correct steps are taken at the appropriate time and in the correct order.

As such Whistle feels that yesterday's meeting was an important step and was the latest in a line of many that they have planned to achieve their objective.

The Prof
Can't help but drawing parallels between Nero and Whistle.
Nero – Fiddled while Rome burnt.
Whistle – Whistle 150-odd questions at the board while West Ham finances burn away to ashes.

Bill, Sydney, Oz
Delusional.

Our Dave
Replacing the chairman is NOT the answer, IMO. Finding someone to invest in the club IS. The Russian from Stamford Bridge is NOT the chairman of that club. He is the major shareholder. That is what we need.

The Joker
Good points raised by Our Dave but I have to say, I don't agree with this 'better the devil you know' attitude. The devil we know has already brought this club to its knees following the largest ever-financial boom in football.

madhammerette

As someone said at the AGM, he doesn't care who owns the club, he is only concerned with how the club is managed and run. Our priority, being supporters of West Ham, is to ensure the club's best interests. But like many others, I don't know enough about company law to know what to do.

In an ideal world, we would have someone in 'charge', who would clearly state their priorities. I mean, if you had a choice two years ago between a new west stand and getting relegated, what would you pick? A museum and a new striker? A hotel and a defender? It's silly, isn't it?

Confused

It's not the thing to support Brown, I know, but do you think he would have chosen the stand over relegation either? Wasn't the idea of the stand to increase capacity, to make us more income, to buy better players, to make us a stronger force?

I'm not convinced about this asset-stripping a struggling club. Why not make us the next Arsenal and then asset-strip?

I thought Terence Brown was totally incorrect when he suggested that 'sometimes you get relegated and it was our turn' but the idea of him somehow cackling and saying, 'I know I'll get us relegated', is totally illogical to me.

FABIO

The downhill spiral can be traced back to the sacking of Peter Storrie and the eventual signing of Aldridge (along with Brown's more hands-on approach). By his own admission, Brown knew little about football. Why did he bring in someone who knew even less?

Redknapp's record whilst in tandem with Storrie was exemplary. Storrie balanced the books when needed and said 'no' to Redknapp. Once he was removed Redknapp had free rein and consequently undid all his previous good work. Since Redknapp left, and under the watchful eye of Brown, the wage-bill rose another £8m or so, contracts agreed and signed by Aldridge became so watertight in the players' favour that the club could not terminate them.

And here we are, five years later, and Storrie has STILL not effectively been replaced! Instead we have two men costing £750,000+ a year, failing miserably to get a grip of the club and point it in the right direction.

Lowell

No-one would invest a penny in West Ham with the current set-up as Brown and his cronies would either give themselves a pay rise or it would be frittered away like all the money from player sales. Remember always that Brown does not have to be chairman even with the most shares. I get the impression from Whistle that one of their suggestions would be to get in someone who has shown an ability to run a company with the turnover of our beloved club – Brown has never shown such financial acuity. If Brown were ever to step down as chairman I would imagine that that would be the time to find a competent and able replacement. Bandying names around now is pretty pointless.

R Milne

I once turned down the chance to partake in a reverse takeover of a much larger competitor because the 51% offered to me would have left me to deal with a belligerent and overfed 49% shareholding. The baggage would put off any serious investor – it's about structure as much as cash.

Alvie

The most effective action against the current board would be a campaign by season ticket holders to defer renewal until the board resigns. If there was an effective campaign, the banks would panic and take the lead in the removal. Despite their good intentions and commendable efforts, Whistle will never gain enough clout with shareholders to achieve such a result.

Joshua

Isn't the whole point of all this is that West Ham, the business, has been run appallingly? This lot, over five years, have lost 50-odd million before transfers in the biggest boom time that football has ever seen.

GEEDEE

That is one of the issues I have with WHISTLE. I keep hearing 'get rid of Brown and the board' and replace them, but WHISTLE don't come up with any names.

Dev

You say that West Ham have no business plan. But what is Whistle's business plan for West Ham? Is the much-needed investment guaranteed?

I applaud all the efforts to date but we need some substantive evidence that Whistle are blowing the right tune, and not just hot air.

Kezza

I think it shows that the main objectives were achieved and we have to be pleased with that.

Claude Du Vall

What a surprise concerning the proxy votes. Are they getting lessons from the Jeb/George Bush School of vote-counting?

cuzoftheeast

I think the intention is replace the chairman with a top businessperson who has a track record of managing a large plc. Said person needn't necessarily be a West Ham fan (it would help) paid on performance against on the field and off the field targets.

The main aim is therefore separation of ownership and management combined with accountability and rewards/penalties for good/bad achievement.

Chapter 11

A THOUSAND WAYS TO BREAK
YOUR HEART
The Play-offs, May 2004

In many ways the First Division Play-off final is now viewed as being one of the highlight matches of the season; it says a lot about modern football that this should be so.

In essence, the Play-offs mean a team can finish sixth in the league, be any number of points adrift from the side finishing third but still get through to a Millennium Stadium final and play in a big game that will receive massive TV and media exposure with the real possibility of gaining Premiership status and the massive injection of Sky TV money that it brings. The total prize of promotion via this route is generally valued at least £20-million to the winners.

There used to be another big game that received massive publicity and promised rich incentives. It was called the FA Cup Final.

In fact, since the inception of the Play-offs no side finishing third in Division One has ever won the final and gained entry to the Premier League, so West Ham were none too sorry when they were pipped to third place by Sunderland.

The Hammers had been in a play-off position virtually all season and although they had a slight wobble in March, they finished the campaign in some style with a number of convincing wins.

The last game of the normal league season was against play-off rivals Wigan Athletic, who needed to win to claim the last available berth. They led 1-0 going into injury-time when a Brian Deane header gained the Hammers a point and allowed Crystal Palace to sneak into the play-offs at the expense of Wigan. If only we had known...

First up, though, was the no small matter of defeating Ipswich Town in the two-legged semi-finals.

BLAGG, May 2004

Regular readers will recall the lack of a Christmas missive from the Blagger last December, as Blagg Acres itself was being relocated along the A12 and my whole life was packed into 82 boxes; 76 of which contained Lady Blagg's shoes.

Being the discerning, loyal and friendly supporters that you all undoubtedly are, nobody emailed me to ask where I was going or why; something for which I am eternally grateful. However, recent events have conspired for me to admit to the ugly truth. You see, for the first time since I was conceived back at the turn of the last century in Plaistow's Maternity Sanatorium, it has now been my unfortunate lot to move away from my beloved East End and its surrounding boroughs.

And do I miss it? Hell, is Iain Dowie ugly? There are a million things I miss: the local Pie Mash emporium, the snug at the 'Fustillian and Bucket', the smell from the glue works, local radio, the Tandoori Hut, the list is endless. What I miss more than ever, though – and this may surprise you – is the reassuring and dulcet tones of LWT's Paul Green.

You see, when the main news splits away for its local update I could always be relied upon for Paul Green to remind me of where I lived. For the most part local news stories were just extensions of national news, protests at Downing Street, tube strikes, rapes in Hackney, drive-by shootings in Stepney, all these things gave me an enormous sense of well-being when I contemplated the capital city that I was fortunate enough to live just east of.

Most people know the 'Big Bang' theory of how the universe was born; few realise that scientists have now pinpointed the centre of that bang as being just two feet from Oxford Street tube station. In short, London is the be all and end all. Everywhere else is just . . . everywhere else.

Harsh? Perhaps. But do you know what the main local *Look East* news event was last Bank Holiday Monday? I swear this is true. A 94-year-old granny climbed 264 steps up a water-tower in Mistley, armed only with a rolled up Persian carpet as an exercise mat and then proceeded to do an aerobic session for charity.

I sat slack-jawed in horror, a sad tear trickling down my cheek, as the camera panned in on this old biddy, lying on her back doing cycle movements and leg splits. Meanwhile Lady Blagg fell off the new sofa in her mirth (she's a Geordie so she sees the funny side of everything).

Anyway, the point of this whole diatribe is that I have to concede that there are several current local sporting news events that are getting on me thrup'pences more than somewhat. No names, no pack drill, but one of them involves a team of yellow and green who have over-achieved this season. I swear if I could have a ten-bob note for every time I've heard ****** Delia Smith praise the fans for their unwavering support; see her wave from the directors' box or hear her twitter (geddit?) once more: "This is the greatest day of my life"; then I could probably afford to buy a riverside house in Docklands and have enough left over for a fish supper.

On the night that the Canaries clinched promotion to the Premiership, the *Look East* reporter actually said: "They'll be dancing in the streets of Norwich tonight". Honestly, you couldn't make it up. Every single evening I'm forced to watch some canary-clad buffoon declare that Norwich's promotion this year is worth about £30m to their company.

But now they've upped the ante. Last night, there was a new threat to my sanity. I knew it was coming, of course, but being forewarned didn't make me forearmed in this instance. For this latest horror wears blue and white and rejoices in the euphemism 'The Tractor Boys'. They play at Portman Road and they want to regain their place in the Premiership at 'the expense of London side West Ham' (sic).

And if they do I may not be responsible for my actions. To watch them 'dancing in the streets of Ipswich' may be more than I can bear. I know we can beat this mob over two legs and all I can do is implore Alan Pardew and the players to do everything to the best of their abilities, rip the gears from their tractors and march on to the Millennium Stadium. To suffer an East Anglian double within six months of being located within its dubious cow-dunged, carrot-crunching boundaries would be the cruellest blow the Great God of Football could possibly inflict on me.

I'll be back after the second leg – providing we're dancing in the streets of Upton Park.

Waily

If I get a ticket for Portman Road, then I'm gonna take my guitar with me. I reckon I should be able to meet up with some six-fingered banjo player and get me some duelling going.

Saracen

I live in what could be the closest place to Hell on Earth if we lose this tie. Diss – halfway between Norwich and Ipswich. Have had the works from the Norwich mob for the last few weeks, and now the Ipswich mob are revving up. And . . . jeeze . . . please not the 'Back Where We Belong – ITFC' banner strung across the A12 again for about two months.

Balto

My wife believes that the centre of the world is Time Square in New York. I have tried to point out to her that the centre of the world is London but she won't have it. If I show her your fine article then perhaps she will believe me.

And for all those of you who moan about TV coverage, try finding out anything about the Hammers in Baltimore!

Wham1966

Good read, Mr Blagg. Reminds me of when I was staying in Bournemouth a few years back and I saw the headline for that day's *Bournemouth Echo*: "The New Wonder Shopping Trolley".

Essex Hammer

I used to live in Clacton and *Look East* used to get right up my nose. They always refer to Ipswich as 'Town' and Norwich as 'City' and when they play each other they take the cameras to some local country pub and interview 'Town' and 'City' fans who are mates with each other. Makes you pine for Millwall and Tottenham.

greenie1

Nice one, Blagg. I'm living on the Suffolk/Essex border. *Look East* and *About Anglia* really do my head in. It's as if Ipswich and Norwich are the only teams that exist in the country. If we win I'm gonna be doing back flips round Suffolk.

Chickenrun

Go on, Blagg 'fess up how far into E. Anglia have you gone? When people ask, I tell them Essex (truth) but the harsh fact is I am far closer to Portman Road than the Boleyn and at work I am surrounded by Tractor boys and girls. Many of my mates are ITFC fans – we have agreed a mutual silence until one week after the play-offs!

cOOL cOL

So where exactly do you live, Blagg?

Billy Blagg

To those asking EXACTLY where I live, I'm afraid I must refrain from revealing my precise location. I am in the Witness Protection Programme and will invalidate my terms of bail if I reveal further.

However, I would like to confirm that I am still in ESSEX (although I'm not sure if this is a benefit or not), so those leaping to the support of Suffolk and Norfolk are wasting their time.

In answer to the dozens of people asking if they should reconsider moving, I'd just say it's 'different strokes'. Some people like the smell of cow dung in the morning . . .

HAMMERDOWNUNDER

My brother moved to Norfolk and worked as a farm hand for a few years. Fortunately he passed away before he had lived there long enough to start growing turnips out of his head.

strong dreams

I live in North Suffolk and was born in South Norfolk. The son of a Cockney and a Geordie! You have to live in these backwaters for quite some time before you realise the benefits.

They mainly consist of liquid refreshment. Green King from Bury St. Edmunds is a good place to start but move up into Southwold for Adnams, then on into Norfolk for Woodfords. After you manage to marinate your liver (Delia-speak) in these heavenly brews for several years, *Look East* takes on a totally different perspective. It's a bit like that 'magic eye' business where you have to concentrate hard on a bunch of colours, then all of a sudden you get it.

Enjoy the rural life, Mr Blagg. Sit behind a tractor or a caravan and contemplate the play-offs. When you do venture back into civilisation you will enjoy it all the more.

Lady hammer

Only 76 boxes of shoes? . . . that's a pittance!

I got into serious trouble when I moved around about the same time as you. I had 'more coats than a chain of Miss Selfridges', much to the old man's disgust!

Anyway, never mind that . . . we WILL be dancing in the streets on Tuesday, you mark my words.

whuami

Is it really that bad there? I'm waiting to finalise a house move, 12 miles from Ipswich, so should I pull out before it's too late?

norwaytips

Now listen here, Blagg, me ol' son. Don't knock my lovely East Anglia, please. OK, Norwich you can have a go at, but leave Suffolk alone. I even have a soft spot for the Tractor Boys. Sorry, I can't help it. I do hope we beat 'em. In fact I hope we crush 'em. As for the dancing in the streets, a couple of pints of good Suffolk ale (Greene King) and you'll be dancing too, Blagg!

X

Is that true about Oxford Street?

GL

What a revelation! I live 10 miles from I*****h and I thought I was alone in desperately needing to beat this lot EVERY time we play them. Forget Millwall or even Totscum, for us exiles this is THE local derby, but now it takes on a much bigger significance. Come on you Irons! Give it everything and we'll be OK, otherwise the rest of my life doesn't bear thinking about!

Couchy

Fantastic. I never realised there were so many people out there who hate *Look East* and *About Anglia*. Please, please, please send the Tractor Boys back to farming their EC-subsidised oil seed rape.

inconsistant fc

I sympathise. I know plenty of Ipswich hate *Look East* and think Stewart White is a **** who should be drowned in pigshit and set on fire.

Chickenrun

Inconsistant, he looks like he already has!

Upton Park Mark

Moved to Ipswich six months back, and live close to our old centre-half Richard Hall, who is alive and well. Unfortunately he's still injured!

Tim A

I live in Chelmsford and am so horrified by the parochial garbage that is BBC East/Anglia that I went to the vast expense of having another aerial put up pointing at London.

I would rather watch the London news through a blizzard than watch crystal clear carrot-crunching from Cromer.

Si.

You must be just down the road to me. It is rather unnerving in my local surroundings, the way that grown men walk around in Ipswich shirts on a Saturday, almost like they are supporting a proper football team (there goes my snobbery again).

Ashy

I'm with you there, Mr B. I am sick of hearing about Ipswich, both on TV and from my scarecrow-like Tractor Boy acquaintances. I fancy us to win in both legs but I will never live it down if we don't beat them.

I would like Anglia to report on our games as I estimate that we have thousands of supporters in the top half of Essex. They report on the MK franchise, after all, and there's only a couple of hundred people remotely interested in them.

ff

I have lived in the area for five years now and can confirm that the inhabitants (those born here at least) are the most insular, inbred, glory hunters I've ever known. Please give us a result!

sploosh

Speaking as another East Anglian exile, I know exactly where Mr Blagg is coming from. The one great advantage of the Ipswich draw, though, apart from their sh!te defence, is that it is only 20 minutes from home, which makes a bloody nice change.

Bob the ball

Bit of advice when in those parts: keep to the road. They'll have you "squealing like a pig, boy" as soon as look at you otherwise.

MS in the West

Brings a tear to me eye, Master Blagg. Where I live the news generally starts off with 'cat rescued from up tree. Fireman Sam hero again'. Then it goes to the trivial stuff . . .

Our Dave

As for that Delia Smith, the sooner someone rolls her in pastry and bakes her on Regulo 9, the better!

Alf Gandhi

Tut-tut, BB. A trite nonchalant with the blatant swede-basherisms, aren't we? PC (picking carrots) apart, thanks for yet another entertaining read. But could there really be another night of Green Street festivities as of old? I'd lift my pint of Abbot Ale to that scenario.

West Ham lost the first leg at Portman Road, 1-0.

BLAGG, May 2004

And what a strange day that turned out to be . . .

I've had some interesting experiences following West Ham over the years but this may well be one of the oddest. I should have suspected something when Lady B and I turned up at the chosen local venue to watch the match on large screen, only to find the place virtually deserted.

Just as I was envisaging the empty pub echoing to my shouts and taunts, the explanation was given: "Our Sky box is broken". Fortunately, another couple of Hammers wandered in and were able to tell us where to go in town to watch the match, so it was hotfoot to the 'Bullock and Badger', where the crowd was split evenly into Tractor and Cockney.

Then, as the match kicked-off, a woman arrived on the back of a cliché. Now either the family affairs of the Suffolk faithful involve a little more inbreeding than even we suspected or it was a 'care in the community' day out. Whatever. This reprobate, wearing an England shirt and frothing at the mouth, proceeded to stand on a chair and scream "Come on Ipswich" at the top of her voice and, more bizarrely, "On the wing, on the wing, one two, one two" at every opportunity – even when the ball went off for a throw-in.

After 20 minutes a large space had opened up around her and the only ones approaching her were a bunch of squaddies trying to wind her up even more.

When Ipswich scored in the second half the blue and white contingent naturally exploded in a frenzy of dancing and chanting but, instead of the expected confrontation between East London and Home County that we could have expected a decade or so ago, a bunch of visiting Colchester supporters started chanting "Essex, Essex" while the Ipswich supporters chanted "Suffolk, Suffolk". So this is the 21st century football factory, eh? An inter-county farming dispute.

When the final whistle blew it was out onto the streets, blinking in the hot sunshine, where I then became a heady mixture of James Alexander Gordon and Stuart Hall, stopping every 100 yards to tell someone the score or give a brief match report. It was both a mixture of pride and awe to realise just how many people support the Hammers outside of East London – surely something only a few Premiership clubs can claim – and just how badly we all want promotion back to the place where we belong.

Lady Blagg had her fill of football by now and she suggested we go for a drive to find a nice country Inn with a local brew and a ploughman's lunch. I was only too glad to get away to clear my head and soon found myself in Constable Country. Parking up outside a suitable hostelry, Lady B and myself were drawn over the road to the local Norman church where there seemed to be something going on. We never found what it was, though, because as we approached to go in, the vicar standing on the steps, having noticing my Hammers shirt, turned to his curate and said quite loudly: ". . . And what was the score at Portman Road today?"

What can you say to a vicar? 'F*** off' seems inappropriate somehow. I'm not sure if there's anything on the statute books for striking a vicar over the head with a verger (verger on the ridiculous?) but I came very close to finding out. Taunting from a man of the cloth must be pretty close to the ultimate humiliation. Or so I thought.

For just a few minutes later, as we walked away from the church, I was surrounded by three 10-year-old girls on cycles who started singing: "One-nil to the Tractor Boys". It's times like this that I think a return to 70s violence is called for; where a sharpened steel comb and a pair of Doc Martens said more about you than any replica shirt ever could.

I eventually took refuge in a pub garden where sanity returned in the form of two or three Hammers who assured me that 'we'll do 'em on Tuesday night'. I hope so . . . I just hope so.

And the football? Well, I was extremely disappointed with our performance. Once again the balance of the side was affected by moving Harewood out to the right and I felt we lost out territorially in midfield. If Connolly and Zamora are fit, then one of them has to sit on the bench as far as I'm concerned. And if Hutchison is ready, then he must start.

Otherwise, my worries are the same as ever. I know it's a pressure game but surely (Chris) Cohen at left-back would help matters while the argument about Tomas Repka just seems to be as contentious as ever. Whatever happens on Tuesday, the full-back situation must be solved over the summer.

My major concern, though, didn't concern any West Ham player. Instead I was worried about the almost imperious defending of Matt Elliott who treated the claret and blue forwards with utter disdain. His whole demeanour suggested 'Been here, done that and against better players than you' Here was proof, were it needed, that experience goes a long way in these games. I'm very concerned that Ipswich will score at Upton Park, so I think we've got to rely on the tactical nous of Alan Pardew and then produce a classic Upton Park night to go through here.

I fear a night of nail-biting may be about to ensue.

North Bank Nelson

Fear not. We have the new song (to the tune of *The Addams Family*):
Me Sister is me Mother
Me Uncle is me Brother
We all love one another
The Ipswich Family

Withnail

Good stuff again, BB. I live in Scotland now so the chance of there being any Ipswich fans in my local is bloody remote. The locals often have 'second' teams down south, and I've even converted a couple to the Hammers. We'll be there in the pub with our West Ham shirts on – me from Dartford and my mate from Stranraer (who just won promotion). Come on you 'Ammers!

Boyatthammer

Many of us have served our time but while work/life forces you away from the East End, it does not let you forget your roots. We all know it is not support but a way of life to follow West Ham. We will be there in mind – believe me – and we live for the next time fortune will smile on us and we can once again walk down Green Street to go to a match and be among like minded people.

EastEndGeezer

Excellent read as usual, Blagg. I reckon we're gonna do 'em in the second leg. I am the most excited I've been for a long time about going to West Ham. The atmosphere is gonna be electric and Ipswich will be in awe. I've already booked the hotel for the final. C'mon you IRONS!

angola

Blagg, have you any idea how annoying it is to read thoughtful, structured prose, while I'm sitting here with my ringpiece doing somersaults? Can't you just say "#!*## COME ON U IRONS"? Show a bit of camaraderie!

gianni

You certainly painted a picture for me here, BB. Not sure it's one I want to look at for long, though. Superb.

bubbleblower

I haven't got any nails left from Saturday. Have to smoke a pack of Bensons instead.

BLAGG, today

One-nil down from the first leg and the stage was set for a classic night under the floodlights at Upton Park. Manager Alan Pardew invoked the ghost of our departed World Cup-winning captain and was rewarded with an atmosphere inside the Boleyn that could have been cut up and boxed. Amidst deafening noise West Ham set about trying to pull the tie back.

Ipswich could so easily have scored after a minute but it was to be the Hammers' night. Two second half goals, the first a superb effort from Matthew Etherington and the winner from captain Christian Dailly, saw West Ham through to Cardiff.

BLAGG, May 2003

Anglia's *Look East* on Wednesday morning:

"Disappointment across the region this morning as Ipswich

go out of the First Division Play-offs . . ."

Yesssssss! So it wasn't a dream! Cue mayhem in Blagg Acres. Disappointment? Not in this fookin' corner of the region, matey! A joyous moment that I will long remember.

I think there's little point in adding to the mountain of comments and postings about Tuesday night's 2-0 win. Anybody who was there knows what it was like and there was enough of us to be able to tell those who weren't. But, for any doubters out there – particularly among the older contingent – this really was a return to days of yore. Ipswich in '86; Frankfurt and Den Haag in '76; it really was that good. I didn't realise you could make that much noise in the Boleyn Ground anymore.

One note of caution, though: I fear we may all be banned next season as I don't think there was one person in that ground who sat down at any stage of the evening.

The job is not done by a long way but, even so, congratulations must go to Alan Pardew and the players for at least giving us this day out. The simple fact is had we been offered this game last January, we would have beamed broadly and looked up the train timetables.

I'm not going to underestimate Palace – particularly as Iain Dowie is looking a top class manager – but we have to believe that this a fantastic opportunity to return to the Premiership at the first time of asking. At least it is now in our own hands.

As I write this I've just discovered that the £70 the club have deducted from my account isn't for the Cardiff tickets, as I had originally thought. It seems in the excitement of Tuesday night I used the credit card instead of the debit card to pay for my two new WHU replica shirts. If we both have tickets, then great, but as I write this on Saturday morning I have no idea if Blagg Jnr and I will be trekking to Wales next week.

Now I'm aware ticket distribution is difficult and must put a stress on the club, and I'm old enough to remember camping outside of Upton Park on a Sunday morning so, on the face of it, this distribution method should be preferable. But not knowing if a postal application to the club's ticket office has been successful before the ticketing arrangements have been passed to Ticketmaster is a sheer nonsense. If I switch between my Online correspondent and IT Consultant hats, then the situation appears even more ludicrous.

It's my belief that every Club Member should be able to log-in to the web site and check their profile to see if they have been allocated tickets. Currently, even if I have two Millennium Stadium tickets allocated via the club-advertised method, I have no way of knowing and I will undoubtedly spend a large amount of time on the phone to Ticketmaster this Saturday for tickets I may already have.

I can go to the Ticketmaster site and put in my membership number but, with the best will in the world, getting a message saying your membership number has not been recognised and having to assume, therefore, that your details have not been passed because you have been allocated a ticket by WHU, is a pretty scary way to go about things.

In case the club isn't aware – although I assume they are – there are a helluva lot of jumpy punters out here at the moment and it's further heart-stress none of us need.

I don't see any reason why the ticket office staff shouldn't be able to open the applications as they arrive and mark on their system where an allocation has been made. From an administrative angle it should also help the club, as members and season ticket holders would be able to amend their address and credit card details on-line. From an IT angle, this would not be an impossible task and would at least put WHU at the forefront of the technological revolution. Cost? About the same as they used to pay Joe Cole a week, I reckon. And I haven't checked this with Alex yet but I reckon we're both up to the task. You know who to email, Mr Brown.

We're now about to embark on one of those delicious weeks where excitement will build and anticipation grows. Everything will be for the best; young children will have rosy cheeks and your cares and woes will seem very small beer indeed. Enjoy it – with West Ham this doesn't come often. It just remains to wish you all luck with your ticket allocation and see you on the coach to Cardiff. I hope.

Did I just say Cardiff? Yesssssssssssssssssss!

Chickenrun

And Lo, it came to pass.

That vicar is probably wondering about his relationship with his boss after last night :-)

BLAGG, May 2003

Through to the Play-off final and a feeling that the whole season was always destined to end this way. After granting a passport to Crystal Palace with their late equaliser at Wigan, the Hammers now found themselves face to face with London rivals managed by a man who, for a time earlier in the season, had been linked with the vacant manager's job at West Ham. Could the Hammers return at the first time of asking?

Errr...no!

In a desperately disappointing game and performance, West Ham once again paraded those maddeningly inconsistent traits for which they are rightly renowned.

Worse for most fans, though, was the manner of the defeat. Trailing to a Neil Shipperley goal virtually on the hour, West Ham seemingly panicked and began to hit aimless balls towards Brian Deane who had replaced all the recognised forwards up front.

The final whistle bought more despair.

BLAGG, May 2003

West Ham United – you gotta love 'em, haven't ya? Did you think they could make you feel worse than you did last May? Of course not? Well, think again sucker!

Let me just firstly start by saying that, on a personal level, as someone who endured 13 hours on a coach, a virtual 22-hour journey from start to finish and a Millennium Stadium experience that begun just three minutes before the teams walked out, that I found it extremely disappointing to discover that I had made the effort to turn up but the team hadn't.

Still, if nothing else, at least Alan Pardew has another couple of pithy sayings to stick on his next T-shirt. How about 'Plan B? I haven't even got a Plan A?'. Or perhaps 'West Ham United – the fans will turn up but the team may not'? Or, better still, 'West Ham United – a thousand ways to break your heart'.

My best mate, Paul, sent me a text on Friday night: 'It's like Christmas Eve, innit?' I could see what he meant; there was a palpable feeling of anticipation and excitement building around the East End all week. Something you could virtually reach out and touch; a real flavour of 1980.

But if last week was like Christmas Eve then, to stretch this tortuous analogy to its limit, the big day presented us with a huge gift we didn't want: crap TV; a row with the wife and the cat running off with the turkey.

Disappointment doesn't even enter into it.

Let's not beat about the bush, Saturday, May 29, 2004 was an awful day in the history of our club, a day full of ironies and paradoxes. Forget about the fact that an ex-Palace player managing West Ham was facing an ex-Hammer managing Palace; forget that only an injury time Deane goal in the last league match of the season enabled Palace to be in the final at all. Forget the fact that an ex-Hammer was 'Man Of The Match'.

Think instead of the fact that at the very last, just when we thought we were going to get something out of a poor season, we reverted to the dross that we have shown for most of the campaign. Think also how those tactical nonsenses that appeared to have somehow worked in the last month were finally revealed to be the disorganised shambles that most of us suspected they were all along.

Think long and hard how the manager that decided to invoke the ghosts of Upton Park in a memorable semi-final then abused those same spirits with a staggering decision that would set poor Bobby a-spinning in his grave. "Well, Saint Bob, we were a goal down so I decided to remove all of our starting strikers, chuck on a big geezer and just lump the ball up to him in true Academy style".

Pathetic.

Also, for those who believe in the fickle finger of fate, some of the incidents on Saturday make uncomfortable reading. If we wondered whether we might have made a mistake letting Jermain Defoe go in the January transfer window, then that decision was brought home at Cardiff.

Even the sale of David James – perhaps the one loss that most of us thought had worked to our advantage – came back to haunt us as poor Bywater failed to hold onto

Johnson's shot.

The real hard and jagged pill, though, is that it looks like, after at long last going outside of the Upton Park family for a manager, we should have offered it to one of 'our own' after all.

My revered editor, Alex, said he didn't want to start a witch-hunt, and in some ways I can understand him, but I'm not so tardy. I'm hurt and angry enough to dig out the ducking stool. It goes without saying that, in a match billed in one newspaper as 'the most lucrative in the history of English football', Terence Brown has managed to blow £30m by selling various players for about the same sum. But criticising Mr Brown is like shooting fish in a barrel. The board at WHU FC are inept and we all know it.

So deep is our disappointment that it barely rates mentioning that some of the players looked nervous and off-colour, with Harewood and Mullins having their worst ever games for us.

What really stuck in the craw, though, was the complete way in which Iain Dowie out-thought and out-fought Alan Pardew, making the Hammers boss look panicky and clueless.

I'm not pretending for a moment that I foresaw this. In fact, I remember being very worried when Dowie's name was touted about when we began a search for our new boss last autumn. Pardew seemed the best man at the time and I've gone into cyberspace print with praise for his supposed approach to the games. But now?

Well, I'd have to admit that Pardew would need to go some way to ever convince me again that he is up for the big role at Upton Park. I've been unsure about some of his purchases and tactical decisions before Saturday but thought I was missing the bigger picture. What I saw at Cardiff scared me big time.

Why was (Jobi) McAnuff not on the bench? What was the point of Brevett taking up bench space if he couldn't come on to replace a player being torn inside out? Why can David Connolly no longer buy a goal? Did we really need Bobby Zamora? Does the manager really believe Harewood is a right-sided midfielder?

Harsh, perhaps, but ask yourself this. Do you think we

would lose again if we replayed the match tomorrow with Trevor Brooking in charge? Hmmm . . . thought not.

It's inevitable now that talk will return to the sale of more of our 'stars' but I'd have to say that the way I feel at the moment, I couldn't care less. We may as well sell the lot and start again because, and I don't know if you have thought of it exactly like this, we couldn't beat CRYSTAL PALACE. And that's what hurts, because I never thought for a moment we'd blow this. It was, apparently, the biggest game in our history and a 'must win' match. But we lost it. Big time. And in truth, I'm not sure if I can hack another season in Division One.

I'm going away to think long and hard about this. I may be some time.

Iron Hammer
Excellent report, BB. Spot on about Pardew, his shirts, his tactics. Brilliant stuff.

Den Watts
I said Pardew was crap hire from the start and got huge abuse from everyone. I hate being proven right but he was awful last Saturday.

Morrissey
There are many things to blame for the latest failure, Brown, Roeder, etc, but player for player at Cardiff, we had the better team. However poor Pardew's 'tactics', our line-up on Saturday should always beat that Palace team. We didn't, so accusing fingers must also be pointed at the players. They've always let us down when it really matters and this is not simply aimed at the team this season. It is, unfortunately, a trait of the club over many, many seasons.

ONE IRON
I truly believe we did not want to go up. It's the first year in the last 10 that we made a profit. We let in a goal after 62 mins and Pardew takes off three forwards on 68 mins. All three would have been penalty-takers (in the event of a shoot-out). It stinks. Do you think that the players gave their best on the day? I think not.

Ali F

Couldn't have written it better myself, agree 100 per cent.
Saturday was appalling. If we can't beat Crystal Palace we
don't deserve to go up. Pardew got his tactics totally wrong
(for the umpteenth time this season) and the players didn't
play, so no great surprise there then.

I am tired of the totally inept way this club is run. I'm not
renewing my season ticket and will stop going to games at
the start of next season. The campaign starts here . . .

Hacko

Saturday. Just about Saturday. I thought that Pardew
couldn't ask any questions that Dowie couldn't answer. And
actually, over the season, we've had far too many mediocre
performances to really have a sniff at promotion. I feel sorry
for Sunderland, they should have gone up as of right. The
play-offs are too cruel.

strong dreams

The rot set in when Defoe was sent off in the West Brom
game and we came completely unstuck. We have never
looked like achieving anything this season. We would
probably have been a complete embarrassment in the Prem
next year (I think Palace will be). Since Harry was shot we
have been in freefall. What on earth was I doing getting
excited about being in a ******** play-off final for? Is this the
best I could hope for? I feel sick to the stomach when I see
our 'golden boys' elsewhere and it has already ruined Euro
2004 for me.

ff

To paraphrase Karl Marx, admitting there is something
wrong is not enough. The point is to change it!

Baron von Evilswine

To be fair to Pardew, there was a bit of the Denmark '92
about Saturday's game. Here was Palace only in the final
due to our generosity, and thus they had the psychology of
thinking they had nothing to lose. We, on the other hand,
had all the expectations of the underdog heaped on our

shoulders. Add to that how much pressure this game
generates anyway and our players had a very heavy
psychological burden going into the game. This is not to
excuse the performance of Pardew or the players on the
day, merely to put the game into context.

Adray

I'm gutted, to be honest. I think you'd be stretched to find
a club who has consistently kicked its fans in the teeth as
often as West Ham. Leeds are the only team that slightly
compare, but three years ago they were playing Europe's
best in the latter stages of the Champions League.

For me, Saturday was a make or break game. Either the
end of an era, or the beginning of an exiting new one. The
West Ham of old is dead, and next season I would be
surprised if there are any players left who wore the Claret
and Blue two seasons back. It's unthinkable that 400 days
ago we had a team consisting of James, Johnson, Cole
Sinclair, Kanouté, Di Canio, Carrick and Defoe (who couldn't
even get in the team) – and next season our prize asset will
be Stephen Bywater.

We really are struggling, and anyone who thinks next
season will be a breeze needs to have a long, hard look at
the club. A top 10 finish is all I expect from West Ham next
year. I've totally lost faith.

I also found myself in Cardiff asking myself – for the first
time in a long, long time – just why I bother supporting West
Ham. I give up thousands of pounds, day after day after day,
get so frustrated and all for what? For a half-arsed team with
a chairman and a board who don't know their arse from their
elbow. The greatest success I've had in 20 years of
supporting West Ham is seeing them lose in a First Division
Play-off final against Crystal Palace. Says it all really.

Norwich hammer

Mr Blagg, superbly written and as close to the truth as you
can get. I was excited about Pardew and what he was going
to do for us and now I am having doubts about him and this
is only six months on. How on earth did he insist on having
Zamora in the Defoe deal? Did he watch him?

Alf Gandhi

The best thing about the day for me (sitting in a WHU pub in Walton) was the pats on the back I received from geezers who appreciated my Bobby Moore 6-inscribed 50s (wrong era, but never mind) shirt. Arrr, those were the days, eh Bill?

The landlord informed me that (the late) Les Sealey had been reduced to tearing his hair out over Bywater's rugby-style kicks into touch. I had to laugh. A 'top drawer goalkeeper' who can't even kick a round piece of leather in a straight line when it's most needed. The mind boggles.

Myself, I was just reduced to a numbed silence at the prospects now facing the club due to an uninspired and dispassionate lot parading themselves in the infamous claret and blue.

Claret&blueblood

Well it's Tues morn and I still feel angry. We couldn't beat Crystal Palace – not Man U, not Chelsea or even Bolton, but fookin' Crystal Palace!

Another year or more in this league is an almost unbearable prospect. Agree about Pardew's tactics. Have always backed him but his insistence on Zamora starting and Marlon on the right, when it has never worked, is alarming.

Also agree about the signings and bench. We purchased two right-wingers, two forwards and two midfielders in a matter of days in January – but no defenders, when it was obvious that we needed them most. Then neither winger appears good enough, although neither got a game, Marlon is shoved on the right to accommodate Zamora (who was not needed) whilst we have average centre-backs playing out of position as full-backs! Brevett surely could have been no worse and at some stage (prob before the final) should have been tried! An all-time West Ham low for me, I still feel sick.

RdUeSpSrEeLsLsed

I'm getting so annoyed with this 'if we had Defoe he would have scored and if James had been there that shot would not have slipped' bollocks. Defoe never wanted to play for us this season and showed it. If we still had him we would not even have been in the play-offs, because if someone don't want to play they won't. James was good and loyal but Bywater has done no less than James did and Bywater is going to get so much better to the point where he will be an England player in the future. WE LOST, that's it, that's what play-offs are about. I'm gutted but shit happens. Let's try and be positive.

Ronald_antly

I was never sure why so many people were so excited when the club stole Pardew from Reading. I wasn't aware of any great credentials he could point to, but at the same time I was prepared to sit back and let him convince me.

Every now and again he did something that made me take notice but the results were patchy. Then, right at the business end of the season, he seemed to be getting more consistency, in the results at least. His tee-shirt at the Ipswich second leg seemed a little eccentric, if not arrogant, but I was happy to go with it as long as the performance and result were right. However, you are setting yourself up for a large helping of 'egg on face' in the event of a defeat.

When he took off Connolly, my heart sank. There was no better illustration of the gargantuan error Pardew had made than when a long ball was flighted to Deane on the edge of the box. He did the job he was presumably on for – that is he nodded it down. However, none of our three recognised strikers were able to sprint from the bench to get to the ball in time.

Hopefully Pardew will have learnt a few lessons from Saturday – and will benefit from them

HQ_Monaro

OK, it is all well and good to find someone to bag because we lost – not because we (the fans) didn't try hard enough but the club let us down. This is true but it just seems to me that every time something doesn't go our way we immediately ask for the manager or a player's head. This is not the answer. A new manager would take the same amount of time to adjust to the players and work out a game plan. Pardew only came on board in October – he needs time.

Sir Alf

We are a decent back four away from a decent team and have been for as long as I can remember. Last time we looked solid and consistent and had back-up in defence was, well . . . err . . . never.

That back four has been the Achilles heel since Charlie Paynter. Stats say we did not let that many in but we always look vulnerable down the flanks and the likes of Dailly and Repka should enter the Olympics in a new event – the 100 meters back peddling race. Dailly has admittedly raised his game following the booing in February but, let's be honest, he has been seriously lacking for several seasons otherwise.

The one time we started to look difficult to beat came when Roeder was forced to play Johnson and bought Brevett the season before. It got us some balance at the back. We need to get those flanks sorted, Mr Pardew!

South Sydney Hammer

Once again, Mr Blagg, you summed up exactly how I feel. Compare Pardew and Dowie. Dowie came to a club in as much turmoil as we were, but with a lot less resources and support. Pardew came to a club that I think most people thought had the wherewithal to go straight back up, and he was blessed with more at his disposal than Dowie could ever dream of.

So why is that we were beaten to automatic promotion, and in the play off final, by a team that, let's face it, shouldn't have had a cat in hells chance? The buck has to stop with the manager on that one, fair and square.

Melbourne hammer

I was just amazed by our style of play for the entire match. I can't remember at any stage in the first half a defender passing to a midfielder, or a midfielder passing to an attacker. And it only started happening after the goal when Connolly, in particular, started making some runs and the ball was played to feet.

It was so dire and I was so peeved – no heart, no tactics no brain and piss-poor football. What a load of rubbish.

snaggletooth

We certainly ended the season on a low note. I couldn't believe what I was seeing for the final quarter of the match – hoofing balls into the box and hoping for miracles. It wasn't even 'hit and hope', it was shit and hopeless. Whatever the reasons for the inadequate display, we, the supporters, are the ones who have to take stick from work-mates, etc, about the non-performance on Saturday. I was almost as sick as I was on the final day of last season. At least there were no tears this time.

In all honesty, though, I'm kinda glad that we didn't make it back up, because I think there was a better than average chance that we could have been looking at some right embarrassing results in the Premier League.

Woody

I'm still gutted from a completely lacklustre performance from most of the team and the sheer arrogance of Pardew. How he can justify the team selection and substitutions is beyond me. I don't agree with the old adage of not changing a winning team. If that worked, then once you win one game you'll win them all. As a manager you have to think of the team and not individuals – why not play a left-back in that position? After all, you've been putting him through reserve games to get him fit.

Why not play the league's second leading goalscorer up front? Don't say he's better on the wing – most of his goals for Forest came from playing up front for Christ's sake. And don't play a striker who needs two or three, even four, touches to bring a ball under control.

Mullins was always going to get mullered at left-back. Harewood has produced nothing in ages on the right-wing and Zamora has lost all confidence, but never mind start them all in the most important game we've had in ages. As for motivating the players . . .

Pardew has failed. He was brought in with the aim of getting West Ham back into the Premiership at the first attempt. He hasn't, so therefore he has failed. Before everyone gets on to me about the squad he inherited, the changes he has made, etc, remember he would have taken the plaudits had we won so he must suffer the criticism in defeat.

I am bitter and disappointed as I have foolishly believed all season that we would somehow do it. That we would bounce back and push on. In reality (and this is what really hurts) we are just an average First Division club with a small minded attitude. We deserve better for our support but will have to accept that Spurs, Charlton, Fulham and now Palace are bigger than us in footballing terms. Christ, even Millwall will be playing in Europe next year.

Crap, isn't it, that 90 minutes of inept football, as dished up on Saturday, can bring you this low.

knob-chops

Mullins looked very anxious and indecisive but Harewood was a liability. So many of you are so hypocritical and so wise after the event. I don't remember many of you suggesting that Pardew should alter the line-up after the inspired semi-final performance against Ipswich.

How anyone could justify Harewood being moved up front when there appeared not even to be a puff of smoke, let alone any fire, in his belly, I will never know. I was surprised by the introduction of (Nigel) Reo-Coker on the right but I thought he did OK. I was also surprised by, and disagreed with, the other two substitutions but they were always likely to have limited impact once Carrick was injured and we were effectively down to 10 men.

Yes, I am bothered by the fact that we misfired on the day, but I don't believe that, over the full 90 minutes, we looked any worse than Palace. Both teams were extremely mediocre. So, to me, all this talk that Dowie did so much better, is fiction. Ultimately, Palace had 11 players who turned up to the match. We had nine! And that, for me, was the main difference between the two teams.

Badhabit

Generally well said, Blaggers, most of which I agree with – you truly are the East End bard. EXCEPT my tee-shirt slogan for yesterday is a mite wittier: "Brooking our place in the Premiership" (BB – You're right, it was).

Oh how I wish he were in charge yesterday. AND – I would NEVER, EVER say "I've had enough of that". WHU till I die,

I'm afraid, and try as I might I can't break a bad habit. Anyway, I KNOW you'll be back. (BB – You're right again).

Tynan
I like your work, Blagg, so I'll stick to posting that knee-jerk rubbish.

Bullybaggio
Totally agree. When will Pardew realise that Harewood is not a midfielder? Pardew needs to have the balls to drop one of them and give us a more balanced side. The support inside the ground was crap.

Clack
Agree with you, Blagg. You can only get away with playing players out of position for so long, a game or two at most. Dowie was able to exploit all our weaknesses, most notably Mullins and Harewood.

You quite rightly make the point that if Brevett was not fit or ready, then why the hell was he on the bench. And if he was fit and ready, why the hell, as an authentic left-back, wasn't he brought on to replace the guy who isn't an authentic left-back and was getting torn apart and ridiculed every time Palace attacked?

Palace's goal came when Repka was caught in two worlds when he had two players advancing towards him, 'cos Harewood was strolling back. But I do not blame Mullins nor Harewood for our defeat – it's not their fault that they're being played out of position, asked to do things that don't come naturally to them and that they're not capable of doing.

RdUeSpSrEeLsLsed
It's going to be fine, you wait and see. We will sell and release players but I'm sure it will not be any of the new ones. There are young players coming through that will be gradually brought in and will not be sold. I personally think we will walk it next season, be better prepared and be run like a Birmingham or Charlton when we are in the big time again. I look forward to next season.

keddy

I've been in exile in the Far East and what really shocked me was how slow and ponderous our movements were. We just didn't seem to play as a team. We looked like a spent force even in the early stages. It looked even worse in Thailand because they put the Holland/Belgium game on before and the players were just light years ahead in technical ability and speed. It was just embarrassing to watch it with the natives.

However, the only smidgen of a silver lining is that these players are simply not ready for the big time. So the youngsters can do with one more season playing the Millwalls, Readings and Rotherhams of this world and then hopefully we'll be ready for the Premiership next year, but make sure we get one of the automatic places. I don't think I can go through that again!

Upton Park=Mecca

Why are we always so forgiving? The night after the match in Cardiff was weird. You could not hear a Palace fan singing anywhere. It was just us celebrating (for what I don't know) and singing 'Bubbles' and 'Always look on the bright side of life'. Could have been going to Old Trafford and Anfield again next year but, no, it's Millmoor and Vicarage Road again for us (sigh).

Lady hammer

Know what? I don't think the board ever wanted us to be promoted. If they did, would they have sold Defoe and James when they did? I think they would have shown a bit more optimism and kept them till the end. I mean, I could just see Defoe scoring on Saturday, couldn't you? In fact, if we had kept him we probably wouldn't have been there on Saturday. I just don't know any more, Mr B. I, too, can't stand the thought of Division One for another season, it fills me with dread.

Sxboy_66

I was quite happy with Pardew's appointment and I'd continued to regard it as, generally, a sound move right up until the quirky tee-shirts. At that point I thought, OK, that's a bit of fun but shouldn't the manager and the team be fully focused on the job in hand? But maybe he knew best.

Then the dogged persistence with which he insisted on playing Harewood on the wing, more doubt crept in. The final straw was the Roederesque panic which led to the substitutions. At that point I knew that my fears were justified. He choked, he ran out of ideas, and he panicked.

It's not a case of 1000 ways to break your heart, though, Blagg. It's more like half a dozen ways . . . but repeating them over and over and over again.

mugabe
The comment about Brooking says it all. Trevor played all of those games last year as if they were cup finals. Pardew seemed to want to put out a 'safe' team. Be honest, didn't you all think that Harewood HAD to play in the middle? How many had confidence that Zamora could lead the front line? Mullins was given a hopeless task by Pardew and why was Brevett on the bench? Waiting for Mullins to break a leg?

cd hammer
The reason why the atmosphere wasn't that great in the ground was because, outside, you had all the real supporters together while inside the ground everyone was split up with the day-trippers, so you only got small pockets of singing. I blame the club again for the distribution of tickets. The crowd I went with applied for a ticket after the Wigan game, thinking we would be with the 'die hards', but instead we got stuck three rows from the back of the third tier with people who wouldn't know their 'Bubbles' from their 'Alan Pardew's claret 'n' blue army'.

alex x
Billy sums up my own gutted feelings. My Pardew rating from Saturday was a generous ZERO.

Thought he should have shown enough bottle to change the side from the last day out with Hutchison fit. Even if you accept his starting line up, he didn't react to make the right changes initially, and then overreacted leaving us without any pattern.

What needed to be done at half-time: Mullins was being torn apart, primarily by being played out of position. Palace know how one-footed he is and exploited it at every opportunity. With the game balanced at half-time, Pardew should have brought on Brevett for Mullins and Hutchison for Zamora, with Harewood pushed up front. Hey, suddenly we would have had a balanced side. Instead, Pardew waited 'till we then went a goal down, and suddenly took off all three strikers in the space of six minutes and brought on two midfielders and a slow, past-it forward!

I couldn't help wonder at the end of the match whether we appointed the wrong manager, Dowie clearly showing an ability to get the maximum out of every player consistently since being appointed at Palace.

alfs barnet

Blagg – You have six weeks before it all starts again. If you're an England supporter, you also get to be let down by your national side during that time. You'll feel a bit better after that.

Let's at least give Pardew the pre-season with the team he's put together before we start writing him off.

cOOL cOL

The crowds outside were superb but for some reason, as soon as I took my seat and play started, I felt that the West Ham supporters and the team were very nervy. At this point I thought, "oh no, this isn't going to be our day".

I was right. Pardew made mistakes, the fans were not as up for it inside the ground as much as they were outside and the players were so nervous they simply didn't play. Everyone must take a part of the blame and now we must just put it all behind us and look to the future. Whether you think that future is bright or not, it is still West Ham.

Come on you Irons.

Oh yeah . . . and BROWN OUT.

CaptainBlueAndClaret

The West Ham Utd players just sat quietly in the dressing room, no one spoke. All that could be heard was a tap running in the dressing room toilets.

There was a whole tray of sandwiches, a pile of sausage rolls and a slab of ginger cake uneaten. Nobody was hungry. The players looked grim faced.

Alan Pardew burst into the room, looked round, opened his mouth as to speak, but no words were spoken. Instead, he looked to the floor, brought his hand to his face, turned and walked out.

Dailly, the West Ham Utd captain, had a plastic cup of tea in his hand. He had only drunk half of it. Dailly threw the cup towards the rubbish bin, but it missed and tea spilled out onto the floor.

Usually this would have drawn some sort of comment, but all knew that this was not the moment. The players just sat there 'stunned'.

Gutted-hammer
Noooooooooooooooooooooooooooo...

OhhhhMattyMatty!
Oh well, always next year.

BLAGG, today
'Twas ever thus with West Ham – "that's it, I can stand no more, they've made a mug out of me for the last time", the litany of the true Eastender. The thinking went on In bright summer sunshine – why don't I do something better with my time? Learn to ride a unicycle, study Chinese medicine, search for the lost chord, split the atom using only a bread knife and a small coffee table?

But all too soon the European Championships were over in Portugal and the national football team had suffered more embarrassment and disappointment. Then the England cricket team stuffed the West Indies, the weather perked up and all of a sudden you more disposed towards team sport.

Finally, the fixture lists are published, and an astonishing fact is revealed. Once again West Ham are no longer in the First Division! In another Football League fait-acompli the old First Division is being renamed the 'Coca-Cola Championship', while Division Two is now League 1 and so on. Nobody need ever finish last any more; all cats are grey *in the dark and your Auntie is your Uncle – terrific stuff!*

West Ham, after a century of trying and failing, is now in a Championship race. Hey, the way things are going, perhaps they will let us in the Champions League, too!

Now the gnawing in your soul begins and the love/hate affair starts all over again. Forget the past, this is a brand new day. Get that replica strip washed and watch out for a bright, highly-motivated team. We have the best manager, the best players and the best set-up. Doubts are for another time.

Another season beckons – bring it on!

Chapter 12

BACK ON THE GLORY TRAIL
October 2004

Is that a light at the end of the tunnel or an oncoming train? At the time of writing West Ham sit poised in what is euphemistically called a 'Play-off place' but a mere three points behind the league leaders. The team claiming top spot has changed at least half-a-dozen times already this season and there is a real feeling that nobody has stamped their mark on the Championship yet. In this sense, the Hammers could be seen to be waiting, poised like a panther ready to pounce. Alternatively, it may be that their claws are trapped firmly in the undergrowth and they are doing nothing other than making roaring noises.

Positive points are the fact that, without playing well, the Hammers are tucked in behind the leaders. In many games they have been territorially superior but have not always been able to turn that superiority into goals. The hope is that, as the season progresses, the club will find that bit of sharpness and creativity to turn possession into points.

The negative side is more concerning, though. Of our best players this season, one comes from our 'parent' club, who have generously loaned us an excellent defender but only for a three-month period, while the other is a 38 year-old ex-England forward who looks unlikely to be able to play the two games a week that this division demands. Beyond that, the Hammers' 'stars' look second-rate.

But should we be worried about how we look in the short-term providing we can gain promotion? This is where the conundrum begins. Some argue the only thing of importance is to get out of the division we are in. After all, there's no point in worrying how we would fare in the Premiership if we're doomed to wander the Championship for a decade or so.

Even so, it's hard not to look at our conquerors in the Play-offs last season and note that they, together with last season's champions, Norwich City, and runners-up, West Bromwich Albion, are finding life hard in the top flight. But that's inevitable, surely? The key thing is that they avoid occupying the bottom three slots at the end of the campaign. Beyond that, little else matters to them.

To that end, though, it's interesting to note the tactics employed by WBA in trying to decide their immediate future. The West Midlands club have taken the tack that getting out of one division and staying in the other are two very different animals. Consequently they have virtually rebuilt their whole squad in the manner of Bolton Wanderers and Birmingham City before them. It will be interesting to see if they can survive. And survival is what this is all about.

At the moment it is only right and proper that West Ham do all they can to try and gain promotion from the Championship but supporters can only sit and wonder what will happen if the Hammers actually achieve their goal. Should we expect that promotion will free up £20m so that the Hammers can reclaim their place at the top table? Will Dale Winton replace Martin Johnson?

There is a horrible feeling of *deja-vu* at the Boleyn Ground nowadays. The days of Mike Small and Leroy Rosenior, Kenny Brown and Paul Hilton, are surely back. The sale of Michael Carrick to Spurs for a sum that seems, frankly, unbelievable (surely even Spurs realise they got Defoe and Carrick for a song – why else would they lend us players?) marked the loss of the last 'crown jewel' and the tragic end of a golden era that never really arrived. The Hammers are now dependant on the generosity of their North London cousin; a club that can now pay £3m for a player only to turn and say: "Ahhh look – you play with him for a while. It's only fair – after all, you gave us that England international (by the way, he's bloody good, isn't he?)". Unfortunately, the loan of Calum Davenport serves to kick sand in the faces of the West Ham fans. It shows what a good central defender can really bring to the club and how £3m can quite easily be seen to be a good investment rather than a waste of a new set of duvets in a Quality Hotel. Rumours that Glenn Roeder has just bought a cat so that he can kick it should not be discounted.

But the chill wind that blows in from the Upton Park Bus Garage can no longer just be put down to seasonal changes and a lop-sided stadium. Attendances (those that aren't artificially boosted by the Kids-for-a-Quid scheme) have dropped alarmingly as fans sense that West Ham are no longer a Premiership side slumming it for a season but are now a *bona-fide* Division One – sorry, Championship – side. Not necessarily a good one either.

Also, it's fair to say that not only is the honeymoon period with Alan Pardew now officially over, but many supporters have even taken to sleeping in the spare room while refusing to make him sandwiches for work.

If there were questions asked after the Play-off final debacle then the first two months of the new season hasn't really answered them. The 'let's be positive' comments are still there and doubtless the training room walls are full of Confucius wisdom and *bon mots* but tactics and substitutions look just as confusing and misguided as they did under Harry and Glenn, so there's no real sense that anything is moving forward.

The style of play is turgid, at best, but, more worryingly, there's no real feeling that the Hammers have acquired someone who can motivate players into performing above their skill level – something that is absolutely crucial at this level of football.

In fact, in the case of someone like Hayden Mullins, a potentially good player is starting to look confused and bereft, not really knowing where he is supposed to be playing nor quite what is expected of him.

Similarly, Bobby Zamora is now starting to wear the haunted look of a man who has suddenly realised that top scorer in League Two may be about his level of incompetence. This is where good man-management needs to assert itself and I'm not sure it will come about by posting a new slogan on a goal post.

I'll put my cards on the table here. American psychobabble

of the type seemingly beloved of our latest boss scares the bejesus out of me. Even assuming – and I think it unlikely – that a 23-year-old sportsman is able to walk past a poster in the training room and see something like: 'Think positive thoughts and be a winner' and stop, ponder and go: "Yeah, that's a good idea, I think I will". Isn't that only going to work once? How many times is he going to stop and look at that notice and think: "Whoa yeah, I forgot about that, I'll do it again today." And hell, shouldn't he be thinking thoughts like that anyway?

And if you're, say, Joey Beauchamp, and you're unsettled and convinced you've made a mistake, is a note blu-tacked to the wall likely to make you change your mind? Do you think Teddy Sheringham needs reminders like these? Isn't the fact that he worked hard and made the best of himself the reason he was successful? You never know, the bloke actually might be talented and have a genuine gift for football. There's an original thought for you – feel free to bung it on a wall somewhere.

Now nobody is naïve enough to believe that these opinions won't all change if the Hammers suddenly find themselves 10 points clear by the end of the year and Alan Pardew is being hailed as the new David Moyes (remember Moyes is the new Bill Shankly) but the chances of that happening seem remote to say the least. And the one area where AP could be seriously challenged – his skill in the transfer market – will have to remain 'under advisement' (as US lawyers say), because lack of funds dictate that Pardew can only look in the *Exchange and Mart* 'Honest Scuffler' section at the moment.

One of the sadder aspects of relegation has been the division of the West Ham supporters themselves. To the older contingent who have grown up on a diet of Devonshire or Parkes, Bonds or Brooking, Cottee or Martin or even Moore and Hurst, watching Alan Pardew trying to coax the best from Marlon Harewood is an extremely painful sight. However, the alarming fact is that West Ham have failed to trouble the trophy engravers since 1980 and a generation have almost grown-up and left home and so their perception of what is happening at Upton Park is entirely different.

For this reason the fans seem to be gathering in two

camps: one are pragmatically accepting that the Claret and Blue are unlikely to bother Arsenal in any foreseeable future and are looking for a niche market somewhere around the Norwich, Southampton or Birmingham area, while others – usually older – are insisting that history has a part to play in what has happened at Upton Park over the past five years and lessons need to be learned in order to move forward.

In that annoying way that often happens, there is some justification for stepping back and thinking both camps have a valid point. But at the moment, it would see West Ham need a spark from somewhere to lift them from Championship mediocrity. That spark doesn't seem to be within the club, so money may be needed to introduce it. But there's no money and without money…well, you can see where this is going.

For some there is an unpalatable truth to be told here because, even in adversity, supporting West Ham United is a great adventure – some might even argue the adventure is *because* of the adversity – and seasons like 2004-05 seem just part of the cycle.

But a part of you just can't help but wish it wasn't always like this.

Bill, Sydney, Oz
What is now important is where we go from here: whether we overcome the pain and disruption of relegation; how quickly we go up and how solid will be our stay when we do go up. Those are the truths about West Ham at this moment in our 100-year history.

And a final truth: we have better attendances than almost all teams in our league and better than (I would guess) more than half those in the Premiership. Money thru' the turnstiles is still an important ingredient in any club's success.

North Banker
Aren't we talking about things by degree here, though? Shouldn't we have overcome the 'pain and disruption of relegation' by now? And it may be that we have 'better attendances than almost all teams in our league' but if they are 5,000+ less than last season, then I would argue that accepting that it's still higher than Reading, Wigan or

Ipswich is irrelevant.

I feel a lack of a credible chance of returning and/or staying are more pertinent issues here.

DavidL

At Coventry away my son said: "Come on, it's not that bad". I reminded him that when I started watching my beloved West Ham I was able to watch Hurst, Moore, Peters and Brooking, to name but a few. I know we still didn't rule the world then but we saw some cracking football (even losing 4-3 to Stoke having been 3-0 up at half-time was a blinding game) and we won the occasional trophy.

I'm sorry, but I find it really hard to get up for the assembly of loanees and fading stars that masquerades as a team with Premiership ambition and potential. I am also fearful that any of our youth stars will start to hit form in case they get 'Johnson'd'.

I'm not asking for European football every season or nearly winning the league, just a return to the days when we believed we genuinely had a chance of achieving these things. It is the potential this club has always had (until recently) to climb these heights that made us an attractive team to watch. At the risk of sounding like the fair-weather fan I have never been, without this potential watching the C&Bs is almost as painful as watching our over-hyped team labour through games and listening to Pardew's latest board-placating drivel to explain away yet another under-performance.

Ozziehammer

I'm afraid that I am equally pessimistic about our future but probably not for the same reasons. You see I group our predicament with every other club in Div One and the bottom 17 in the Premiership, notwithstanding that Man U are temporarily in that group. What is the point? I remember when you started a season not knowing who would win the league. You knew we wouldn't, although once or twice in 45 years . . . but it might be Liverpool or Forest or Arsenal or any one of a dozen candidates but there was expectation, even for a poor, addicted Hammers fan. But what of now? Does it really matter if we go up? We'll most likely come straight back down. If we don't, we sure as Christ are not going to make any sort of impression for the next 10 years. But then again, neither is any side other than Arsenal, Chelsea and Man U. Money is what it's about now. Forget where we went wrong, it simply doesn't matter. I sit up and get the scores on TV at 3.00am in the morning because I'm programmed since birth. I can't bring myself to believe my own rhetoric but unless we get a benefactor with squillions, it really doesn't matter if Pardew or Jesus Christ is manager. Sorry.

Badhabit

As much as it's tempting for all of us to reel off the litany of disasters that our Board of Misrule has visited upon us since Mannygate, I reckon it's important to see the bigger picture.

For many years since childhood I had harboured the illusion that West Ham was 'my' club, which was merely 'run' and held in trust on my behalf by a bunch of relatively rich Hammers enthusiasts with hearts of gold. Like many fans, I think it took the bond scheme to force me to open my eyes. Nothing I have seen since can convince me that 'my' club is anything but another example of a shoddily-managed British company falling to bits in the face of the forces of global competition. More recently, however, I have ceased to glance enviously at the lot of the Arsenal supporters as they watch the fate of another bunch of Christians thrown through the gates of the Coliseum, or the Chelsea supporters trying to make out just who is the latest blinged-up multi-millionaire who has scored the only goal of the game. A life-long Arsenal fan recently confessed to me that it's only the European games that give him a buzz anymore, to which I replied: "Then why don't you lobby for a breakaway Euro league, to stay there and let the rest of us have our game back?" The truth is that the lucrative football market has gone through the same processes as all other markets. Having been de-regulated and opened up to forces of competition, there has emerged the usual corporate giants at the top of the food chain who then proceed to exert power to re-regulate in their favour. The product they're selling is sanitised, TV- shaped and served with ads for cars, loans and Coke. It bears no resemblance to the sweat-stained, mud-and-guts matches laced with flashes of sublime skill and excitement on a winter's afternoon that we were brought up on.

I don't doubt, however, that I am in a minority; most Hammers fans long for the arrival of our oil-rich Abramovich clone Messiah and a stream of foreign-made team components – just to return to the days of a more balanced world when we could sometimes cream the Spurs, trounce Chelsea and even occasionally beat Arsenal. As for me, however, I just want our game back in some league competition where we can stand on the terraces, enjoy the quality of the soccer safe in the knowledge that we can never predict the outcome, and we can survive on the back of the gate receipts that a crowd of around 26,000 should enable us to. Where is that place?

I read today about 100 towns around the world in the Cittaslow movement (Aylsham is one such) whose citizens have kicked out the chain store and other delights of post-modernism and pledged to live a slower pace of life. Perhaps the West Hams, Wolves, Leicesters, Sunderlands, and indeed even the AFC Wimbledons of this world, should pledge to do the football equivalent, and kick out the super-rich clubs and create a niche market for 'real fans'.

BarrowBoy
Two things:

1. WHU are one of about 10 yo-yo clubs (created since the big TV money came to football). Sunderland, Leicester, Leeds, Wolves, WBA, Norwich are others, with Pompey to join in the next year or two. Focusing purely on internal affairs to explain the situation is too narrow a way of looking at it.

2. Look at the websites of these other yo-yo teams (and the way these clubs go through managers). The excess of bile mirrors that of the WH supporters. The problem seems to be that nowadays no-one can accept anything less than 'success'. This is the result of the wider view in society, where everyone's expectations are too high and, as a result, there is no toleration for anything less than getting exactly what is demanded. There is also a tendency to see conspiracy when it is normally just the usual 'cock-up' that

has occurred. No-one tolerates mistakes any more.

Alf Gandhi

BarrowBoy makes some interesting comments in perspective of the changing societal values at large. We are living in a system that increasingly demands instant gratification and success. Billy represents some of the old dignified West Ham values, borne out of a kind of East London fatalism, at being the poor relation to the rest of the great metropolis. Always standing proud even if the industrial smoke did blow east, we always had more about us than the North, South and definitely the poncier West of London. Our relative past successes and pride was based on our humour and abilities. But never from the unrealistic expectations that seems to define the new breed of West Ham supporter.

But it's not this 'poor little sparrer' self-definition that has seen the demise of West Ham United as a symbol of all that was best in football world full of cynicism. It's poor management and shifty deals in a time of economic rationalisation gone mad. The lack of adjustment to the needs of the corporate capitalism that now controls practically everything from MUTV to sponsorship of Sunday League teams in Botswana has seen our seemingly all embracing demise.

Simple really, you can't sell our best assets and still remain a team with realistic ambitions. And the appointment of Roeder, coupled with the failure to secure the services of either McClaren or Curbishley, has been an almost terminal final nail in an already lowering coffin.

I think that the jury is still out on Pardew – but may be returning soon to deliver their verdict. Although a Messiah he's most definitely not. We could equally scrape promotion as become another Sheffield Wednesday.

FU Chairman Brown

The thing that puzzles me is, I look at the surrounding areas of the West Ham catchment towns and villages seeing nothing but a growth fan base possibility, unlike that of most well-supported clubs. For example, Man U have Man City right on their doorstep, Arsenal have Spurs, Chelsea have

Fulham, Southampton have Portsmouth, Liverpool have Everton, Bolton have Blackburn, Villa have Birmingham and West Brom, Newcastle have Middlesbrough.

West Ham United could say Charlton, at a stretch, but it is over-the-river and not really seen by the Kent people as a thing of passion.

Moving out towards Essex and its borders, there are Southend, Colchester, Cambridge and way up Ipswich for WHUFC to contend with in terms of fan base growth. Any positive-thinking businessman would look at those areas surrounding the glorious Academy tradition of WHUFC and just see future players and fans.

My point is that a cracking WHUFC team, firing on all cylinders in every competition including Europe, would probably attract consistent crowds of 50,000+ – if you bear in mind the 32,000 who turned up at Upton Park to see WHUFC beat Bradford City on a Tuesday evening last season!

When you speak of waste, please bear in mind the wasted potential in not only losing the next young Beckhams from our doorstep but the future generations of fans who will grow into being Arsenal, Chelsea or Spurs supporters.

Brown and the board should be lined up and shot for the Decades of damage they have engineered over the only English club to provide so consistently to the national team and the last English club to field an entire team of English players in a winning FA Cup side. There is a reason why so many English players and the English game have had roots at West Ham including the momentum that Sir Alf Ramsey adopted for the 1966 World Cup winning team. That is because the area has HUGE potential for FOOTBALL.

Sadly, not in the hands of the IDIOTS on the WHUFC board, who are plainly blind except for their own personal ambitions.

twinhammer1

It is really beyond the bounds of possibility for any club with so many well educated directors, some of whom have the experience of being entrusted with the management of our club, while others have been there all of their adult lives, to somehow manage to maintain a level of incompetence for so long. I believe we have all asked how this could have been allowed to happen and why our directors have invested heavily in failure.

Ask yourself why.

I believe that the ultimate plan is to sell our services to another club – these plans have already been commissioned and have started to unfold.

It is planned that the Casino will become the larger part of West Ham. The Academy makes a profit and will continue.

Meanwhile we plan to trial the use of our first team matches for former greats and/or accomplished, ageing players and to nurture young stars of the future. The players' wages paid by the loaning club.

The incompetence is a smokescreen for a downsizing to sell the bits they want to themselves, and have some sort of arrangement with other club(s).

How do we stop this? I don't know, but watch closely as it unfolds.

Herbie Hammer

As an observation of the direction of the club, unfortunately I would have to say that there has been a decline in the fantastic atmosphere at the ground, and the manner of the support – so much so that many only follow the C&B to away games where the support is so much more genuine and positive.

Sorry to sound negative, I still back the boys 100% and sing my heart out at the games I attend, but as a reflection of the club as it is now, I think this is important.

Still, while there's a West Ham side, there is always hope!

cOOL cOL

Whatever happens to West Ham most of us will never stop supporting them. We can gripe and moan as much as we like but nowadays, whether we are in the Premiership or the Conference, we would moan anyway. It is the way we are now after being treated to a club so run-down by Mr Brown that we accept we are a dodgy team with a (so some would say but not me) slightly dodgy manager and we accept we are now a poor club that is likely to become poorer each season.

There was a time when booing, moaning and griping hardly existed and it shows what our club has become when it is now a common occurrence.

We moan, but at the end of the day we accept it, albeit grudgingly, because, as Blagg said, 'even in adversity supporting West Ham United is a great adventure'.

Roll on the next great adventure that we can share with our beloved West Ham.

Twist & Shout

I've come to terms that we are a Championship side with a big club name.

We dont deserve to win this league, we don't deserve to stay up IF we get promoted and as for AP becoming a ledge, it's odd-on that he won't.

But just say he does get us promoted and does keep us up, it will be because of one man and one man only – he has had no backing to bring in top players to get us out of this league. There is no money in the near future, he has had to sell England internationals and reduce the wage bill.

Everything is against him, including the fans, as many think we have the right to go straight up. The truth is, this is one of the hardest leagues to get out of. At least 10 teams are in the mix for promotion throughout most of the season and every game is a battle.

The amount of pressure on AP is unbelievable.

Krap not Pu

My only fear, as was shown in last season's Play-off final, is that too many of our players lack the heart/desire to make it to the Promised Land – ie the Premiership. Knowing full well they are not good enough for that step up, they are content to remain pretty big fish in a small pool.

D.Rollo

Krap, I'd be astonished if that was true of the majority of our squad. If there's one thing you can rely upon about the modern footballer, it's ego. I reckon almost to a man they think they're good enough for the Prem.

Frankie

I'd bet on Pardew getting the boot by the end of next season.

Scribbler

My view is that we won't score enough goals to win the title. Remember Man City got over 100 in their year and Pompey another load, losing only six games.

We average only a goal a game while the Tractor Boys average two. Nuff said.

I don't think either three-touch Bob or the Lumbering Harewood can raise their game. The only decent striker is Teddy Sheringham.

Of this squad, few could play in the Premier. Perhaps NRC, Sheringham, Bywater, Fletcher. That's about it except for Ferdinand and Cohen.

So would the board sanction the purchase of six-to-eight players? More importantly, could Pardonme actually go out and identify them?

Answer to both questions is . . . NO.

Bedford Rascal

The only cert is that Pardew will get the sack. If the team continues its patchy form and shit performances, he'll soon be under pressure.

If we don't get promotion he'll be on his way.

And if we do, then we'll have a humiliating season in the Premiership and come straight back down – he'll get the bullet then.

Chapter 13

THE BLAGGERS CRYSTAL BALLS

In many ways the future of West Ham United FC is inextricably linked to the very fabric of English football and the future of every club that isn't fortunate enough to ply its trade in the Champions League every season. If you only get your dose of football from the tabloids and TV coverage then you may be astonished to find that this is actually the vast majority of professional league clubs.

There have always been successful clubs and what the Americans call 'die-nasties'. Tottenham, Liverpool, Nottingham Forest, Arsenal, Derby County, etc, have all had their day in the sun. It's probably even fair to say that West Ham have had their own bit of sunshine over the years, too. Arsenal or Man U dominating the league isn't anything new but that isn't where the problem lies. The current difficulties of West Ham and clubs like them can be traced to the virtual emancipation of clubs not in the top four or five and the dire consequences for those who drop out of the top sector.

It wasn't always so. Where it all started to change, though, was with the advent in August 1993 of the FA Premier League and, more importantly, the expansion of the absurdly named 'Champions' League.

Once upon a time, when referees wore top hats and footballs had laces, if you won the top division then you were called Champions and allowed to enter the European Cup. This competition pitched the champions from every European country against one another in a knockout competition, and it was interesting stuff.

However, there was a major drawback for the clubs involved and that was that one lack of concentration on a cold night in Bratislava and that was your lot for another year – and that couldn't be allowed to continue. Pressure from the big guns such as Manchester United, Real Madrid, Barcelona, Inter, AC Milan and others demanded that this wasn't 'fair' and if they weren't allowed to keep the ball then they wouldn't play any more. Mutterings about setting up an independent European league were mooted and authorities became worried.

Consequently, the European football authorities under the guise of UEFA bowed to pressure from the big clubs and introduced the Champions League, guaranteeing a divisional series of six home and away matches for the title winners of every league before the competition entered a knock-out phase from the quarter-finals onwards. This assured major TV exposure and gate revenue and was fine as far it went – but what if one of the big boys actually missed out by not being champions of their own country? It wasn't fair to exclude them, was it?

In a staggering piece of re-branding that Gerald Ratner should have copied, the Champions League allowed the league runners-up to enter the competition. Later, the third placed clubs were allowed in and then, to howls of laughter from anyone with any sense of propriety, the fourth placed clubs in certain nations were invited to join the Euro gravy train.

Think on that for a second and then wonder why the Olympic committee don't give medals for athletes coming in fourth. Why not have a Tin Medal? In fact, why stop there at all? Why not have plasticine medals for anyone who bothers turning up in a pair of shorts and a sweat band?

Whatever the arguments, everything was in place to ensure that, barring the end of days itself, Inter Milan, Manchester United, Real Madrid and others were virtually assured of participation in the Champions League every season.

Now you had a guaranteed money-spinner and a competition that any top player worth his salt simply had to play in. The death knell sounded for any club, however big, who had no chance of getting into the premier European competition. Put simply, if a club has a top player who wants to represent his country then he has to play for a club in the Champions League. So if your club have no chance of getting into that exclusive elite, then rest assured any such player will only be wearing your shirt for a season or two. Unless Jacques Santini pulls a spectacularly large rabbit out of the blue and white hat, Spurs fans may well not want to get shirts with the name Defoe printed on the back.

The history of the Champions League, though, is now set in stone and there will be no going back. However, there are further repercussions brewing. Firstly, the little knot of clubs below the top strata are all asking questions about UEFA's secondary competition, the UEFA Cup. This competition used to be known as the Inter-Cities Fairs Cup and included clubs who finished just below the champion sides, a kind of 'also-rans' trophy. With the expansion of the Champions League, clubs finishing sixth or seventh are now being awarded places. But this is still a knock-out competition, a duff night – as West Ham had against Steaua Bucharest back in 1999 - and it's all over for another decade.

Already questions are being asked as to why the UEFA Cup can't be expanded to a league format and other clubs – perhaps as low as 10th – can't be allowed to enter. This question becomes even more pertinent when you consider that clubs knocked out early in the Champions League are allowed to enter the UEFA Cup at third round stage. In 1999 again, Arsenal, the eventual runners-up, actually entered the competition after West Ham had been knocked out! One can only hope that organisers of the London Marathon are reading this, as I am very keen to get a medal and reckon I can manage the last 100 yards.

It is really not stretching the imagination to view a time when the top four clubs from the Premiership, Spain's *La Liga*, and Italy's *Serie A* will enter the Champions League while the following six clubs enter the UEFA 'League'. In essence, the UEFA League is just a long throw away from becoming fact, ensuring that any club finishing in the top 10 of their respective top division will be guaranteed six games against European opposition and cementing a dozen or so clubs to the pinnacle of professional football in their home country.

But it gets better. Following on from the lacklustre showing of the major football nations in the 2004 Euro Championships and the 2002 World Cup, together with the tragic death of former West Ham favourite Marc-Vivien Foé from a heart attack while playing in the Confederations Cup last year, the world and European football authorities have become concerned about player 'burn-out' from playing too many competitive games, together with worries about long-term player injury.

Consequently, there are already moves afoot to force the individual European football authorities to reduce the number of games they play in their top division – probably by the time of the 2008 European Championships. A top limit of 14 clubs to a division is mooted meaning, possibly, that if the UEFA League ever gets off the ground, then only three or four clubs in the top division will be not be playing European competition in the mid-week period.

This last suggestion is the next big battlefield and make no mistake, there will be serious repercussions if there is any attempt to stop a Tottenham or Everton from playing a Liverpool or an Arsenal.

But, from there on, the only answer is a Premiership Division II with everyone else cast adrift as not good enough. With West Ham currently in the 'adrift' position, where does our long-term future lie?

As Harry Redknapp insisted on telling us at every opportunity, "We're not an Arsenal or Manchester United" – and I don't think that's anything that even the most dyed-in-the-wool Hammers fan would disagree with. But, as I urged frequently at the time, let's not worry about who we aren't. Let's think instead about who we are.

So who are we? Well, in the aftermath of the Premiership and the Champions League, it's easy to forget that there are not that many English sides who can claim to have won the FA Cup three times since the mid-60s and less still who can claim that they have appeared in two European finals. This doesn't actually place the Hammers among the pantheons of Real Madrid and Liverpool but, with all due respects to supporters of the relative clubs, we're not exactly a Gillingham, Crewe or Bury either. Hell, can Birmingham City or Charlton Athletic even make such a claim?

Obviously, historically our highest-ever placing of third in the old Division One in 1986 isn't likely to bother the statisticians too much and supporters of clubs such as

Leeds United, Derby County, Nottingham Forest and Aston Villa may well resent our attempts to puff out our chests and muscle in on territory that, by rights, isn't really ours.

Nevertheless, top division status, cup wins, European success and international representation should buy us a few bonus points lost in the pell-mell of league success and, prior to our relegation in 2002-03, I don't think there are fans of many clubs who would deny us a place at the same table occupied by the Southamptons and Villas of this world. With the decline of two of the original 'Big Five', Spurs and Everton would consider a sixth or seventh placing in the Premiership to be a major result nowadays and it's not stretching the imagination to suggest that's where West Ham should be sitting at the moment.

But in fact, looking at the Premiership in 2004-05, you might be wondering if there isn't some type of minor revolution going on in the English league; a place where Birmingham, Charlton, Fulham, Bolton Wanderers and Middlesbrough could probably all regard themselves as mid-table top division sides. You don't have to have a memory that goes back to when Alan Devonshire last jinked down a wing or Pop Robson last headed in at a far post to recall when West Ham might consider a mid-table First Division game to mean when Coventry, Derby, Forest or Sheffield Wednesday came to visit. Now all those sides are playing outside the top division and, in some cases, the way back looks long and perilous indeed.

The difficulty for any club outside the Premiership lies in the loss of the Sky TV money and the buying power it brings. This is exacerbated by the terrible misnomer of the 'Champions' League and the stranglehold that the top sides have on the game. The erosion of the local fan base usually leads to the ubiquitous jokes about Manc supporters from Devon. But that target is almost too easy; consider instead the young kid growing up in Barking who now supports the Arsenal.

It's an old cliché, I know, but in football, as in life, the rich get richer and the poor get poorer and whether or not this is worth losing sleep over is a matter dependent upon which side of the fence you sit. However, for the fans, unlike real life, being rich or poor in football isn't a matter of upbringing and opportunity, birthright and education but for the most part, simply a matter of choice. Leyton Orient too dull for you? Hey, don't worry! – Liverpool are on the TV next Wednesday (and the Wednesday after that and the Wednesday after that . . .) so why not just buy a shirt and support them? You can look on a map another day!

Back in the days when Dr Martens were found on the feet of supporters rather than across the chests, if you wanted to see the fans of Manchester United, Liverpool or Newcastle United then you had to attend the home match when you played that opposition and then look over to the away end. Now, you can pretty much walk down any high street in the country and guarantee seeing at least five different replica shirts before you've completed an afternoon's shopping.

The depth to which this situation has sunk was brought home to me during a work discussion about Euro 2004. One of my colleagues mentioned that her young son had been allowed to stay up to watch France as he 'supported them'. I suspected not, but couldn't help enquiring if his Dad was French "No, it's just that France have a lot Arsenal players playing for them, so he supports them". This was a frightening argument in itself but the conversation took an even darker turn when I was told that her son had argued: "Anyway, there's no point in supporting England as they never win anything".

What a depressing future that conjures up. I mean, why bother supporting Oldham Athletic and England just because you were born there, when you can support AC Milan and Brazil?

Some may say this is the power of TV and the might of the marketing men and it's an argument that would probably stand up to close scrutiny, so the response must be to play the game to the agreed rules – and it's here where our beloved club has come unstuck time after time. Because the unpalatable fact is that West Ham United has not only missed the boat but they have closed down the docks, mined the water and bricked up the roads leading down to the quay.

When England won the World Cup in 1966, the Hammers trio of Moore, Hurst and Peters helped confirm the club as one of the glamour sides of English football. Bobby Moore epitomised the modern sportsman like no other and his clean-cut, fashionable image made him one of the icons of the 60s. With Moore at the pinnacle, West Ham could have cemented a power base that should have survived today and seen us rubbing shoulders with Liverpool and Arsenal – but the small family club mentality ensured this was never done and over the ensuing decades there has been an almost embarrassing apology of ineptitude to stop the Hammers from ever being the club the strong and loyal fan base deserve and expect.

Apart from the head start that West Ham could have had as a modern, progressive football club, the simple logistics of locality should also have ensured the claret and blue were among the top players in the marketplace. If you base Upton Park on a top triangular point in East London and then fan out in either direction below it, then you get a startling demographic of West Ham's possible catchment area. Apart from the obvious areas of East London, Essex borders and the areas beyond, the advent of the fast A13 road and the QE2 Bridge could even serve to bring in large parts of Kent. Nobody is attempting to lure away fans from Gillingham, Southend or Colchester but whole swathes of Essex and Kent should be swayed to West Ham United as their 'big' club of choice. Watching an altercation recently between a Man U and an Arsenal fan in Colchester High Street brought home just how far the club have slipped in recent times.

The really galling thing about West Ham's lack of application and progress over the years is that, for the most part, those clubs who have invested heavily have capitalised on their investments.

Nobody is pretending that running a football club is going to be like investing in Microsoft but there is certainly an argument for the maxim 'speculate to accumulate' to apply and it's interesting to see how the expenditure of a club like Newcastle United has paid dividends. Doom merchants may point to Leeds United as a shining example of what could go wrong but what makes the Upton Park situation unique is that, unlike the Yorkshire club, West Ham has never had to bid large for a Defoe, a Lampard, a Rio or a Johnson, Cole or Carrick – those players were already at the club. All we had to do was to hang onto these players and try and build round them; invest in a quality manager who could persuade the players that staying at West Ham was a viable option and build a professional, progressive outfit that represented the community it was rooted in.

Instead we took the quick buck and the easy way out and then found there was a trapdoor outside the exit.

One of my abiding shames is that, as a season ticket holder at WHU for five seasons some years back, I was asked by questionnaire if I thought the club should stay at the Boleyn Ground. Ever being a traditionalist where football is concerned I answered 'Yes' – and I was wrong!

After the 1989 Hillsborough tragedy and the Lord Justice Taylor report, West Ham United FC should have found a purpose-built new home in Docklands. As it is the Rio Ferdinand Stand, Quality Hotel and Museum, soon to be gambling casino and probably – by the time you read this – bordello, stands as a monument to poor investment. Doubtless there are accountants and board members who can successfully argue otherwise but my blood runs cold whenever anyone speaks about loan repayments.

And don't forget work on the other (east) side of the ground isn't even being contemplated at the moment, giving us a lop-sided ground with no atmosphere. For anyone who stood on the North Bank when we played Den Haag and Fintract Frankfurt in the 1076 Cup Winners' Cup it's enough to make you cry.

Whatever way you look at it, this looks like a club going nowhere and only the manager and players can change that because, whatever else we have to do, the slow crawl back is only going to start when we are back in the Premiership, where we undoubtedly belong. Do we have the coaching in place and the players to lift us back to those lofty heights? Don't ask me. I thought a team containing Di Canio, Cole, James, Carrick, Sinclair, Defoe and Kanouté was too good to go down – so what do I know? This isn't about individuals but it's about an elusive whole.

Because for me, the last five years of West Ham United are a microcosm of the club's history. For Mannygate read lack of professionalism; for the Rio sale read lack of belief and small-mindedness; the subsequent investment of the Rio money makes for poor decision-making and investment and lack of control at the very top; the sackings of Redknapp and Roeder indicate poor timing and bad man-management; while the misguided belief that relegation could be avoided in Glenn Roeder's second season suggests an alarming inability to face facts and do whatever has to be done – cowardice, if you will.

And even where it has come right – the Intertoto success of 1999, Roeder's seventh place and reaching the Play-off final last season – that aforementioned lack of leadership at the very top means that, for want of a brave move, decisive decision and, dare I say it, a few bob here or there, we have been left wanting. Yeah, we've not always had the rub of the green – going down with record points hauls and virtually identical consecutive season results serve to point that out - but, as the Fergusons and Wengers of this world will tell you, you make your own luck. And we make ours bad.

The depressing thing about all this is that Mannygate was just part of an ever-turning circle. I could probably write another book about the record-breaking 1985-86 team and the ill-fated bond Scheme or another about the 1975/1976 teams, and Bobby Moore's excellent autobiography is essential reading to recall what happened to the legendary 60s side.

Despite accusations in some quarters, I'm no apologist for the current chairman and board but you have to understand that this is like filling in cracks and painting over the repair work when the whole structure needs underpinning. In 1921, there was uproar in the East End when local hero Syd Puddefoot was transferred to Falkirk for £5,000 – then a record fee. I've no doubt Mr Brown's predecessor said: "It was an offer we couldn't refuse". In fact, I've got this horror film picture in my head where, were I to see a photo of the WHU board in 1921, then like that picture of the Jack Nicholson character at the end of *The Shining*, they would all be the same as today except for Brylcream and a beard. Perhaps then manager, Syd King, refused to let Puddefoot go proclaiming he was 'down to the bare bones', locking himself in the dressing room until the chairman broke it down with an axe: "Terry's here!"

This club has been shaky for a long time and a major structural change needs to take place because otherwise –

and we hope it's not one day soon – the whole thing will fall down. That change may come through natural development or it may come via Arab oil, Russian roubles or a good old Cockney entrepreneur (please). But something has to change because otherwise this cycle will repeat itself.

The fact is if we could get a crystal ball and next week bring in a large group of promising 18-year-olds who we know will one day pull on an England shirt, then we can rest assured that none of them will be representing us by the time they are in their early twenties.

Don't get me wrong, though. I'm no rattle-waving believer of the 'Good Old Days' (there weren't many of them anyway). I'm quite able to get a steely glint in the eye and get all General MacArthur about things, waving a fist and yelling "We'll be back" – especially if we're playing Ipswich Town.

And I believe we will be back – probably sooner rather than later, too. I see nothing to suggest we're going to do a Sheffield Wednesday. But I'm also a pragmatist. I don't see any future that won't involve me looking back to the Ferdinand/FLJ/Cole/Defoe/Carrick era and thinking, "Hell, we blew that big time".

And this club and its supporters deserve better because at West Ham United the one thing that we don't have to check; the one thing that we know is strong and will prove to last forever are the rock-solid foundations based around the fantastic Hammers support. The one place where West Ham can claim to be in the Premier League and striving out into the golden lands of European success is on the terraces, where the Claret and Blue faithful are quite simply second to none. There may be the odd Scouser, Manc, Geordie, Gooner or Russian Billionaire who picks up this book and says: "No way – our fans are better". To them I say: "Come back and see me when you have been relegated, seen your side lose 6-0 and 4-0 in a semi-final and cheered like a loon through both and then seen your side decimated through stupidity and poor investment – then we'll talk".

My guess is that they won't be back.

It's easy to be a good fan when you're winning things and being feted on every sports page and every football show. To put up with the type of thing that West Ham fans have had to endure over the past few decades is another matter. I'm reminded of the punch line to the age-old joke. St Peter at the Pearly Gates: "West Ham supporter? Come in – you've suffered enough!"

My abiding hope is that before any of us gets to meet the Big ref in the Sky we can all look back and celebrate some success and that we can comfortably pass the claret and blue baton on to our grandchildren, as my grandfather did to me.

It's not much to ask, is it?